QUICK AFTER-WORK
CHINESE
Cookbook

QUICK AFTER-WORK
CHINESE
✤ Cookbook ✤

KIT CHAN

PIATKUS

First published in 1998 by
Judy Piatkus (Publishers) Ltd
5 Windmill Street, London W1P 1HF

ISBN 0-7499-1797-0

Photographs by Peter Cassidy
Styling by Helen Trent
Food prepared by Kit Chan
Text designed by Paul Saunders
Step-by-step illustrations by Rodney Paull and Paul Saunders
Decorations by Paul Saunders

Typeset by Action Typesetting Limited, Gloucester
Printed and bound in Great Britain by Bookcraft Ltd, Midsomer Norton

CONTENTS

INTRODUCTION

CHINA IS A VAST COUNTRY, bounded by barriers of ocean and mountain ranges that tend to segregate people to certain areas or regions. The four regions are: Northern (Beijing, Shantung and Honan), Eastern (Shanghai and Fukien), Western (Szechuan and Yunnan) and Southern (Canton). Each of these regions has developed a distinctive style of cooking which often differs greatly from those of its neighbours. In describing these regional cuisines, there is an ancient and well-known saying that goes: 'South is sweet, North is salty, East is hot and West is sour.' And much of this still runs true today.

Of the four regions, the Cantonese style has gained the most popularity in the West – the first Chinese restaurants were opened by emigrants from Canton and from the neighbouring British territory of Hong Kong. There is another reason why Cantonese food has been so celebrated. When the Ming dynasty was overthrown in 1644, the imperial household and many government officials fled from Peking to Canton, taking their chefs with them. These chefs assimilated recipes on their way south and took advantage of Canton's rich produce – and combined these innovations with their native Peking style of cooking to make Cantonese cuisine the most original in China.

The Chinese adore food, and spend many hours shopping for the finest ingredients. They know that fine cooking begins at the market, that to cook well is to buy well. And to buy well is to select ingredients not for cost alone, but for freshness and quality. Once at home, these ingredients must be prepared. Almost like matchmaking, the cooking method most suited to the ingredients must be found so that each brings out the best in the other and counterbalances any deficiency. The aim is to enhance and complement their natural flavours, but always to keep their appearance so that they are beautiful to look at and their clarity and freshness are emphasised.

A Chinese meal consists of several dishes, which usually include a meat one and fish or seafood and vegetables as well as soup, rice and tea. There is a great togetherness in the way the Chinese eat. There are no separate courses – the entire meal is set out on serving dishes at the centre of the table. Each diner can see how much food there is and partake of the meal in communal style. All the dishes are shared, with the exception of rice; this is served in individual bowls which can be refilled. Chopsticks are used.

Since there is no single main course you may wonder how many dishes to serve if you are planning a Chinese meal. There is no hard and fast rule. In general, plan as many dishes as there are people to serve: two dishes for two people, and so on. But adapt this to your time and budget; you may want to cook fewer dishes, but in larger quantities. A dish can be stretched by serving it with more vegetables and rice. Most of the recipes in this book serve four people on their own or six to eight with other dishes in a Chinese meal.

Chinese cooking can be economical as rice, and wheat in the form of noodles, are China's staple diet. The addition of meat, fish or vegetables is a luxury dictated by economic circumstances. Meat is used in small quantities, cut up or finely sliced and often combined with several other ingredients, making a little go a long way.

The recipes in this book are a selection of some of the easiest and quickest dishes to make, and take into consideration the fact that in these modern times we are increasingly occupied with work and careers. Chinese cookery is a world full of aromatic aromas and flavours. With a few basic store-cupboard ingredients, and a flair for improvisation, it is much easier than you may think. In short, good fresh ingredients are always the key and by combining these with the authentic use of seasoning and spices you can re-create delicious and distinctive Chinese meals in your home. You can, of course, enhance the recipes through trial and error to suit your taste.

INGREDIENTS

Chinese cooking calls for ingredients which are both familiar and strange. As Chinese cuisine has become more popular, more manufacturers have gone to great lengths to make them supermarket items. Good Chinese cooking, however, does not depend on rare and unusual foods, but on understanding ingredients, knowing how best to prepare them, using treatments like marinating – and finding the best cooking method for them. The basic ones that give Chinese cooking its characteristic flavour and taste are soy sauce, fresh ginger, garlic and spring onions. In addition, there are a number of special spices, sauces and seasonings that will transform ordinary ingredients into dishes of great interest.

Here are a few essential ingredients. Although many may seem expensive, they are used sparingly and will go a long way.

Bamboo shoots
Young, tender and ivory coloured shoots of an oriental plant. Used as a vegetable, they add sweetness, delicacy and crispness to soups, seafood and poultry dishes. Occasionally available fresh, more commonly available canned – whole, sliced or in chunks. The whole shoots packed in water, not in brine, are best. Bamboo shoots should always be rinsed before they are used.

Bean paste, brown
Thick, spicy, aromatic paste made from yellow beans, flour and salt which are fermented in a semi-mash. It adds a salty, full-bodied flavour to food.

Bean paste, yellow
Salty, pungent paste made from ground soy beans. It is used to flavour and preserve food and is sold in cans or jars.

Black beans, fermented
Small, black preserved soy beans. Extremely strong, pungent and salted, they heighten the flavour of meat and poultry.

Cabbages
There are dozens of varieties of Chinese cabbage. The following are the most commonly available.

Bok choy A tender, delicate vegetable with long, smooth, milky white stems, topped with crinkly green leaves. The entire vegetable is edible. It has a clear, light taste and requires little cooking. It is available year-round. There is also a baby bok choy now in the markets, which is about 15cm (6 inches) long. It is rather delightful and is very popular in trendy restaurants.

Chinese or Napa cabbage Oval shaped, about 25–30cm (10–12 inches) long, with crisp, tightly packed leaves. It is sweet tasting and very nutritious. Can be eaten raw in salad, but primarily used in stir-fry dishes and soups.

Gai lan Slender, green stalked, rather like broccoli. The flowers in the middle of the plants are white, with a slight bitter taste.

Mustard green A sturdy vegetable, dark jade green in colour with tightly packed leaves that are curved, fluted and fan-like. It is slightly cool and bitter tasting. Use in soup and stir-fry dishes. Can also be braised, and is very good for pickling.

Chillies

Chilli peppers are used as a hot seasoning, primarily in Szechuanese cooking. There are many different kinds of chillies. In general, the smaller the chillies, the hotter they are. The fire comes from the seeds, so discard them if a milder flavour is preferred. To prepare, break off the stem with a small knife, cut the chilli in half lengthwise and scrape out the seeds, then cut away the fleshy white 'ribs' from each half. Chillies contain volatile oil that can irritate the skin and cause eyes to burn. Always wash your hands after handling them, or you could wear gloves while preparing them.

Chilli sauce or paste

A piquant seasoning made of crushed chilli peppers, vinegar and assorted other seasonings, including garlic.

Chilli sauce, sweet

Sweet, garlicky and spicy hot, this bottled import from Thailand is quite new to the market. Use as a dipping sauce or condiment.

Dried shrimps

Tiny dried pink and white shelled shrimps. They enrich the flavour of tofu, cucumber and cabbage and must be soaked in warm water for 10 minutes before use.

Hoisin sauce

Thick, dark brown, savoury, sweet and tangy, it is made from soy beans, spices, garlic and chillies. It is also known as barbecue sauce.

Mushrooms

Cloud and wood ears   Small, dried, charred-looking fungi. They must be soaked in warm water before use and will expand to five to six times their original size and become meaty and succulent. After soaking for 20 minutes, rinse well to get rid of any bits of bark or grit, and trim off hard or woody stems. They are much appreciated for their gelatinous and crunchy texture.

Shiitake   Also known as black mushrooms, these are brownish-black with caps about 1–5cm ($^{1}/_{2}$–2 inches) in diameter. Meaty, succulent and savoury, they can be stir-fried, braised or simmered. To use, rinse in cold water, then soak for 20–30 minutes in warm water. Drain, squeeze dry, then trim off the stems. Use the caps as required, and save the stems and soaking liquid for stock.

Mushroom soy sauce

A seasoned black soy sauce flavoured with dried Chinese mushrooms. It has more depth and roundness of flavour than soy sauce. Use in stews and sauces.

Noodles

Cellophane noodles   Made from ground mung beans, these are also known as bean thread, transparent, glass or pea starch noodles. They are dried, wiry and white looking. Cellophane noodles must be soaked in warm water for 20–30 minutes before cooking.

Egg noodles   Egg noodles are made from wheat flour, egg and water. The dough is flattened and then shredded or extruded through a pasta machine to the required shape and thickness. These are available fresh or dried.

Rice vermicelli   These thin brittle noodles look like white hair. Rice noodles are purchased dried. They are best soaked in warm water for 20 minutes. They can be deep-fried.

Wheat noodles   Sometimes called Shanghai noodles, these are made from wheat flour, water and salt. They are made in the same way as egg noodles but are whiter in colour. Available fresh or dried, and in varying thicknesses.

Oyster sauce
Thickish, slightly sweet and salted brown sauce made from oyster extract, soy sauce, sugar and vinegar. It is used to flavour all sorts of meat, fish and vegetable dishes.

Plum sauce
Piquant and thick, amber-red chutney-like sauce made from plums, apricots, chillies, vinegar and sugar. It is used as a condiment or in stir-fries.

Preserved cabbage
Pressed, salted and dried mustard greens. It is used to flavour soups, stews and steamed dishes.

Rice wine
Made from fermented rice. This all-purpose Chinese wine can be used in cooking or consumed as a beverage. The most commonly known is 'Shaohsing' wine, which can be purchased in Chinese supermarkets. If Shaohsing wine is not available, a medium to dry sherry, or even whisky, can be used instead.

Sesame oil
An aromatic, nutty-flavoured oil extracted from roasted sesame seeds.

Sesame seeds
White sesame seeds are frequently used in Chinese cooking for added flavour and texture. They are easily available in most supermarkets and health food stores. Black sesame seeds are more rare, and are used to make a sweet pudding and for decorating and garnishing. Both types will keep for several months in an airtight container.

Soy sauce
A thin, salty, savoury brown sauce made from soy beans, wheat, yeast and salt. It comes in many grades and types ranging from light to dark, thick to thin, and is an essential background seasoning. Unless a recipe specifies otherwise, use dark soy sauce. This has been aged for longer and is richer than the lighter variety.

Szechuan peppercorns

These look like black peppercorns with small seeds. They are mildly hot with a pleasant aroma.

Toban sauce

A thick, spicy paste made from garlic, chilli peppers and soy beans. This pungent mixture is very popular in Szechuan cooking.

Vinegar

Vinegar is widely use in cooking as well as for dipping sauces. Chinese vinegar is usually made from rice. There are many varieties ranging in flavour from spicy and tart to sweet and pungent. Cider vinegar is usually a good alternative to rice vinegar.

Water chestnuts

Fresh water chestnuts have the texture of a crisp apple and are delicious raw or cooked. They add sweet flavour and crunchy texture to dishes. When fresh water chestnuts are not available, canned water chestnuts are the best alternative. Already peeled, they lose flavour and crispness during processing, but still add texture to dishes.

Wonton wrappers

Wonton wrappers are very thinly rolled sheets of wheat flour and egg dough. They are available ready-made in packets, either fresh or frozen. If you can't get them, use spring roll or filo pastry instead, although the results will not be quite the same. Once you have opened a packet of wonton wrappers, keep them covered with a clean damp tea towel to prevent them drying out and turning brittle.

THE CHINESE KITCHEN

You don't need a new kitchen or elaborate equipment to cook Chinese food. Ordinary pots, pans and utensils will do. The Chinese use three basic utensils: the wok, cleaver and chopsticks. But if you are looking into new equipment, here are a few suggestions.

Wok

An all-purpose cooking utensil, round in shape with high sides. It distributes heat evenly and allows ingredients to be stirred and tossed without spilling. Woks come in a range of sizes; if you have an electric cooker, it is best to choose one with a flat base. You can add a dome-shaped lid. Woks are useful for steaming, braising and stir-frying.

Cleaver

Another all-purpose Chinese utensil, this looks like a butcher's cleaver. There are several kinds: Stainless steel cleavers look good and are easy to keep, but carbon steel ones have a better edge and are easier to sharpen – but they will rust if not properly looked after. Lightweight cleavers are used for slicing. Heavier ones can be used for chopping bones and their handles are useful for pounding and mashing.

Chopping block

A good, strong, heavy wooden block is useful.

Chopsticks

These are quite versatile and can be used instead of wooden spoons, forks and whisks. Wooden chopsticks can withstand high temperatures.

Steamer

The Chinese use special steamer-pans which are set in tiers, one on top of the other, over boiling water. A lid on the top pan contains the steam. The pans can be made of metal or bamboo. You can use as many tiers of steamer as there is food to be cooked, so this is an ingenious way to steam several different dishes together, using the same water and heat.

Spatulas and draining spoons

There is a variety of spoons, ladles and spatulas for different jobs. For stir-frying, a long-handled, shovel-like spatula is used to stir ingredients or flip them around the wok. A deep-frying basket, strainer or slotted spoon is used for deep frying.

Rice cooker

An electric rice cooker can be costly, but if you eat a lot of rice it is a good investment. It has two switches, one to cook and the other to reheat or keep warm. You simply add washed rice and water and the rice is cooked automatically. The cookers come in a range of sizes and non-stick ones are available. I find these excellent as it means there is no need to scrape and wash the bottom of a burned rice pan. Using a rice cooker also leaves a cooking ring free.

PREPARATION AND COOKING TECHNIQUES

Cutting

Chinese cooking requires a fair amount of preparation in the kitchen. Chinese people like to cut meat and vegetables in small pieces of the same size and shape. This not only looks attractive but helps the items to cook quickly when stir-fried in a wok, which helps them retain their crispness and fresh flavour. Also, because knives are not traditionally used at the dinner table, it is essential that the pieces of food are small. You will need a good sharp knife.

Shredding   Some recipes require the ingredients, usually meat or vegetables, to be cut into very thin strips. To do this, vegetables should first be washed and peeled and meat and fish should be trimmed of all unwanted matter. To shred vegetables, cut a thin strip from one side of the item so that it lies flat on the chopping board. Cut crossways into 5cm (2 inch) lengths, then cut each length into thin vertical slices. Stack up the slices and cut them lengthways again into strips. Meat should be cut into slabs about 2.5cm (1 inch) thick, then cut each slab across the grain into strips. Now cut the strips into shreds.

Chopping   Chopping consists of cutting ingredients into small dice. Then, with a large knife, cut in one direction, then another, bouncing the knife up and down on the board until the ingredient is chopped as finely as you like.

Deveining shelled prawns

Prawns have a thin dark vein running down the back which must be removed. Often you can just pull the vein away gently. Otherwise, make a shallow impression along the back (outside curve) of the prawns with a small knife, then ease out the vein with a cocktail stick. Rinse the prawn under running cold water, drain and pat dry.

Dry roasting

Dry roasting spices or seeds releases their aromas which will then permeate the dish you use them in. Heat a wok or frying pan until hot. Add the spices or seeds and stir continuously over low heat for about 2–4 minutes or until you can smell their roasted aromas.

Stir-frying

Stir-frying is the method most often associated with Chinese cooking. Essentially, it is cooking food in a small amount of oil over high heat, stirring constantly so the food is never in contact with the cooking surface long enough to burn. Vegetables retain their natural colour and texture, and meat and seafood come out tender and juicy.

Stir-frying is a very quick process, and the key to it lies in the preparation: chopping and cutting ingredients into bite-sized pieces to make for rapid and even cooking; soaking dried ingredients; and measuring any other ingredients so that you have everything to hand before you start to fry. A lot of this can be done beforehand.

When you are ready to stir-fry, heat the wok until it begins to smoke, then add the oil, pouring it in a circular motion along the rim of the wok. The heat of the wok will heat the oil almost instantly. If the recipe calls for ginger and garlic, these are usually added first and allowed to sizzle for 30 seconds in order to flavour the oil. Then the main ingredients are added – together or in stages depending on whether some ingredients take longer to cook than others. The principle is that the harder the ingredient, the more heat and time it needs. Ingredients must be added to the wok in sequence so that their cooking is completed at the same time. This sounds more difficult than it actually is. A few drops of wine or sherry may be added to enhance the flavour of the food at this point. The contents of the wok should be turned over and over with a shovel or spatula until cooked.

Deep frying

Foods for deep frying are usually cut into medium-sized pieces, then coated with flour or batter. They are then immersed in deep hot oil until done. This process seals in the flavour and ensures that the food will be completely cooked in the middle and crispy on the outside.

The correct temperature for most deep frying is around 170–180°C (325–350°F). A Chinese cook usually tests the temperature by placing a bamboo chopstick in the hot oil. If bubbles form around the chopstick, the oil is ready. If however the bubbles form very fast, this indicates that the oil is too hot. You may of course test the temperature with a special thermometer or with a piece of stale bread – if the bread turns golden in 60 seconds, the oil is hot enough. Items to be deep-fried must be completely dry or they will splutter dangerously. Don't overcrowd the pan or you will reduce the temperature of the oil too much and the food will stick together, take much longer to cook and soak up too much oil. Once cooked, the deep-fried food is removed from the oil and drained thoroughly on absorbent kitchen paper.

Steaming

Steaming preserves the natural juices and flavours of food. You can steam food in a wok or a pan by placing a flat, perforated metal 'steam plate' or a rack stand above 5–7.5cm (2–3 inches) of water. Bring the water to the boil, then arrange the food to be steamed on a shallow dish and set this on the steam plate or rack. Cover and start timing. Be sure that the water continues to boil throughout. Remove from the steamer when still slightly undercooked, as the food will continue cooking in its serving dish even after it has been removed from the heat.

As a rule, the steamer should be opened as little as possible during cooking, but if the steaming period is lengthy, additional boiling water may be added from a kettle. If using a stack of steamer trays, the order of the trays should be reversed midway through the steaming period.

APPETISERS AND SNACKS

T HE CHINESE have the habit of eating many small snacks throughout the day, more often than not on the street or in the marketplace while shopping. The food is often transportable and is prepared by street vendors and at roadside carts as well as in snack shops.

The supply of these quick and easy snacks seems endless, and their variety is staggering. They range from a bowl of hearty soup to elegant steamed dumplings, or fried treats like wontons and prawn toasts.

In China, starters as such are not usually eaten before a main meal. The dishes on the following pages can be served as snacks or appetisers at drinks parties, but will also make excellent entrées for a Chinese-style dinner party. The delicious dipping sauces that are often served with them add an extra dimension to their exotic flavours.

Paper-Wrapped Chicken

THIS IS A popular Szechuan method of deep frying. Small pieces of meat or fish are marinated, then wrapped in greaseproof paper and deep-fried until tender. To eat, break open the packets one at a time with chopsticks or a fork. You can make larger packets for a main course. I like to keep them small and serve them with other appetisers.

——— MAKES 12–16 SMALL PACKETS ———

350g (12oz) chicken breasts,
  without skin
1 tablespoon chopped fresh ginger
2 garlic cloves, chopped
1 tablespoon soy sauce
2 tablespoons hoisin sauce
1 tablespoon medium-dry sherry
greaseproof paper cut into 16
  approx. 15cm (6 inch) squares

a bunch of spring onions, cut into
  short lengths
50g (2oz) canned sliced bamboo
  shoots, rinsed and drained
50g (2oz) peas
oil for deep frying
salt
freshly ground black pepper

1. Cut the chicken into 5cm (2 inch) cubes. Combine the ginger, garlic, soy sauce, hoisin sauce and sherry. Toss the chicken with the mixture and leave to marinate for at least 10 minutes.

2. To assemble, put a square of the paper in the diamond position and place one piece of chicken together with a couple of pieces of spring onion, some bamboo shoots and a few peas near the bottom corner. Season with salt and pepper. Fold the paper and wrap it into a packet: fold up the bottom corner to cover the filling, then fold up again to form a triangle; now fold the left and then the right corners towards the centre, like an envelope; finally, fold the top corner down like an envelope flap, and tuck its end in securely. Repeat to make 16 packets. The packets must be wrapped carefully so the oil does not seep in. This you can do a few hours in advance and then just deep-fry when you are ready to eat.

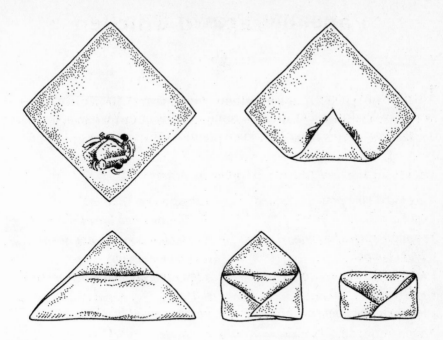

3. Heat the oil and deep-fry the packets in batches until done, about 5 minutes. Drain and keep warm in a low oven until all the packets are cooked. Serve hot.

Sesame Prawn Toasts

THESE VERY popular snacks are not only good as starters, but also as canapés with drinks. For the best result, use bread that is a couple of days old as it makes spreading the prawn mixture easier.

—— SERVES 4 ——

225g (8oz) king prawns, shelled
   and deveined
5 canned water chestnuts, drained
   and chopped
1 teaspoon chopped fresh ginger
1 egg white
1 teaspoon medium-dry sherry

1 teaspoon cornflour
4 slices of white bread
2–3 tablespoons sesame seeds
oil for deep frying
a few sprigs of coriander or parsley
salt
freshly ground black pepper

1. Mince or process the prawns, water chestnuts and ginger to make a paste. Add the egg white, sherry and cornflour, season with salt and pepper and blend well.

2. Divide the mixture evenly and smooth it over the slices of bread. Sprinkle with the sesame seeds and trim off the crusts.

3. Heat the oil. Slide in a slice of the bread, sesame-side down, and deep-fry until golden and crisp, then turn over to the other side and finish frying. Drain on absorbent paper. Repeat with the remaining slices.

4. Trim if necessary and cut each slice into 4 or 6 pieces. Arrange on a plate and garnish with the coriander or parsley.

Bird's Nest Meatballs

MEATBALLS have universal appeal. I like to serve these with a satay sauce or sweet chilli dipping sauce at drinks parties or as appetisers with other dishes like Crispy Seaweed (see page 29) and Sesame Prawn Toasts (see page 16).

—— MAKES ABOUT 30 MEATBALLS ——

450g (1lb) minced pork
1 teaspoon chopped garlic
1 teaspoon chopped fresh ginger
*4 canned water chestnuts, drained
  and chopped*
2 tablespoons light soy sauce
*25g (1oz) breadcrumbs or matzos
  meal*
1 egg, beaten

*2 tablespoons chopped spring
  onions*
*2 tablespoons chopped coriander
  leaves*
3 tablespoons cornflour
115g (4oz) dried rice noodles
oil for deep frying
sweet chilli sauce

1. Combine the pork, garlic, ginger, water chestnuts, soy sauce, bread-crumbs or matzos meal, egg, spring onions and coriander in a large bowl. Mix well.

2. Take some of the mixture into the palm of your hand and squeeze it into a ball, or take a teaspoonful of the mixture and roll it into a ball. Lightly coat with cornflour. Repeat until the mixture is used up.

3. Break the noodles into 1cm ($^1/_2$ inch) lengths. Roll the meatballs in the noodles to coat all around.

4. Heat the oil. Deep-fry the meatballs in batches for about 30 seconds until the rice noodles puff up. For each batch, remove the meatballs from the oil, turn the heat to low and then return them to the pan and fry gently for another 3 minutes. Test one meatball for doneness by cutting it open. If the meat is cooked, remove and drain on absorbent kitchen paper. Serve with sweet chilli sauce.

Vegetarian Fried Wontons

THIS VEGETARIAN version of fried wontons is made with tofu, fresh ginger and spring onions. These days, as well as the standard pork filling, you can use your imagination and come up with your own version, like fish or even a mixture of cheeses. Serve these wontons with the Soy Dipping Sauce below, or with plum sauce or sweet chilli sauce.

—— MAKES ABOUT 25 WONTONS ——

1 tablespoon pine kernels
2 tablespoons sunflower oil
1 tablespoon grated fresh ginger
2 teaspoons chopped garlic
a bunch of spring onions, chopped;
   reserve 1 tablespoon for the Soy
   Dipping Sauce
225g (8oz) firm tofu
1 teaspoon sesame oil

1 tablespoon soy sauce
25 wonton wrappers
1 egg, beaten
oil for deep frying
a few sprigs of coriander
salt
freshly ground black pepper

Soy Dipping Sauce

2 tablespoons soy sauce
1 tablespoon sesame oil
1 tablespoon rice vinegar

1 teaspoon chilli oil
1 teaspoon honey

—————— ◆ ——————

1. Dry roast the pine kernels in a small pan for 2–4 minutes until they turn golden brown. Leave to cool, then chop them.

2. Heat the sunflower oil in a frying pan. Add the ginger and garlic and fry for 30 seconds until fragrant. Add the spring onions and fry for a further 30 seconds.

3. Crumble in the tofu and stir-fry for 4–5 minutes. Add the roasted pine kernels, sesame oil, soy sauce and salt and pepper to taste. Remove from the heat and set aside to cool.

4. Meanwhile, make the sauce: Combine the soy sauce with the sesame oil, rice vinegar, chilli oil, honey, 1–2 tablespoons water and the spring onions in a bowl, and mix well.

5. Place a wonton wrapper on a clean board or surface in the diamond position. Take a spoonful of filling and place on the centre of the wrapper. Brush the top edges of the wrapper lightly with beaten egg and pull the top corner down over the filling to make a triangle. Press the edges to seal. Place on a flat tray and repeat with the remaining wonton wrappers.

6. Heat the oil for deep frying. Slide in the wontons a few at a time and fry for a few minutes until crisp and golden brown. Remove with a slotted spoon and drain on absorbent kitchen paper. Fry the remaining wontons. Serve at once with the dipping sauce, and garnished with coriander.

Chopped Chicken Livers

IT WASN'T until recently that I was asked to make chopped chicken livers to serve with drinks at a dinner party. I was quite pleasantly surprised at how good they tasted. Here's my version with some Eastern touches. You can serve them on crostini or crackers, and they are also delicious tossed with noodles or wrapped in crisp lettuce leaves.

—— SERVES 4 ——

1 tablespoon pine kernels
3–4 tablespoons light olive oil
2 shallots, chopped
2 spring onions, chopped
1 teaspoon chopped garlic
1 teaspoon chopped fresh ginger
450g (1lb) chicken livers, cleaned
  and trimmed
a pinch of five-spice powder

1–2 tablespoons rice wine or
  medium-dry sherry
2 teaspoons soy sauce
1 tablespoon oyster sauce
1 hardboiled egg, roughly chopped
2 red chillies, seeded and chopped
  (optional)
salt
freshly ground black pepper

————— ◆ —————

1. Dry roast the pine kernels in a small pan for 2–4 minutes until they turn golden brown. Leave to cool, then chop them.

2. Heat 1 tablespoon of the oil in a frying pan. Add the shallots, spring onions, garlic and ginger and fry gently until the mixture softens. Remove from the pan and set aside.

3. In the same pan, heat the remaining oil. Season the chicken livers with salt and pepper and stir-fry over a high heat for 2–3 minutes to seal and brown. Reduce the heat to medium and cook for another 2–3 minutes, keeping the liver still pink inside. Season with the five-spice powder, then stir in the rice wine or sherry and stir to scrape up and dissolve any particles and juices sticking to the bottom of the pan. Return the shallot mixture to the pan and add the soy sauce and oyster sauce. You can serve the livers like this with noodles or as a filling, or go on to the next stage.

4. Coarsely chop the livers by hand or in a food processor. Serve on crostini or crackers, garnished with the chopped egg, pine kernels and the chillies, if using.

Firecracker Butterflied Prawns

THESE PRAWNS are delectably tempting, with their contrasting flavour and texture. They are also quick and simple to prepare.

—— SERVES 4 ——

2 teaspoons sesame seeds
1 teaspoon black sesame seeds
24 medium-sized king prawns,
  shelled
8 wonton wrappers
oil for frying
2 shallots, sliced
2 cloves garlic, crushed
½–1 teaspoon coarsely cracked
  black peppercorns

2 tablespoons lime juice
2–3 tablespoons sweet chilli sauce
4 spring onions, cut diagonally into
  thin slices
2 tablespoons coriander leaves
2 red chillies, seeded and finely
  sliced
salt

—————— ◆ ——————

1. Dry roast both kinds of sesame seeds in a small pan for 2–3 minutes until they turn golden and give off a fragrant aroma.

2. Cut the prawns down the back about halfway through and remove the veins. Open the prawns out flat and rub with a teaspoonful of salt. Leave for 5 minutes then rinse and drain.

3. Cut the wonton wrappers in half diagonally and fry in hot oil until lightly browned. Drain on absorbent kitchen paper.

4. Heat 2 tablespoons oil in a wok or large frying pan until very hot. Add the shallots, garlic and prawns and stir-fry until the prawns change colour. Stir in the pepper, lime juice and sweet chilli sauce and toss. Add the spring onions and sesame seeds. Check for seasoning and add salt to taste.

5. Garnish with the coriander and chillies. Serve with the wonton crisps.

Steamed Scallops with Ginger and Black Bean Dressing

SCALLOPS steamed this way in their shells for a few minutes until they are barely done are delicious and succulent. You can serve them simply, with a drizzle of soy sauce and oil, or with a ginger and black bean dressing as I have done.

—— SERVES 4 ——

4 tablespoons sunflower oil
1 teaspoon chopped fresh ginger
1 tablespoon fermented black
  beans, rinsed and roughly
  chopped
2 tablespoons chopped red pepper

a pinch of sugar
1 tablespoon light soy sauce
1 tablespoon oyster sauce
12 scallops in half shells, cleaned
2 spring onions, finely chopped
2 tablespoons coriander leaves

1. Heat the oil in a small saucepan. Add the ginger and black beans and stir until fragrant. Remove from the heat and add the red pepper, sugar, soy sauce and oyster sauce.

2. Put the scallops in a single layer in a wire or bamboo steamer and place over a wok or saucepan of simmering water. Cover and cook for a few minutes, or until the scallops turn opaque.

3. Spoon the sauce over the scallops and sprinkle with the spring onions and coriander.

Spinach Salad with Dried Shrimps

Dried shrimps are tiny, pink-white, shelled prawns that are salted and dried. You can use them in a variety of dishes to enrich them. They are especially good with tofu, cucumber, aubergine, cabbage and spinach.

—— Serves 4 ——

50g (2oz) dried shrimps
450g (1lb) spinach
1 teaspoon English mustard
1 tablespoon rice vinegar
2 tablespoons soy sauce
1 teaspoon sesame oil

a pinch of sugar
4 tablespoons groundnut oil
2 shallots, finely sliced
2 cloves garlic, finely sliced
salt
freshly ground black pepper

1. Rinse the shrimps and place them in a small pan. Barely cover with water and bring to the boil. Turn off the heat and leave the shrimps to cool in the liquid, about 10 minutes. Drain.

2. Meanwhile, blanch the spinach in a pan of boiling water and refresh immediately in cold running water. Drain well, squeezing out all the water from the spinach. Roughly chop the spinach and place in a bowl.

3. Make the dressing: Combine the mustard, vinegar, soy sauce, sesame oil, sugar and 2 tablespoons of the groundnut oil and season with salt and pepper.

4. Heat the remaining oil in a small frying pan. Add the drained shrimps, shallots and garlic and fry until golden.

5. Toss the spinach with the dressing and drizzle the shrimp mixture on top.

Sesame Chicken and Cucumber Salad

THIS DISH originated in Szechuan and is also known as 'bang bang chicken' – it used to be necessary to pound or bang the bird to soften the flesh and make it tender. Today's chickens need no such treatment. If you prefer a more intense sesame dressing, substitute 2 tablespoons of sesame paste or peanut butter for the mustard.

—— SERVES 4 ——

1 tablespoon sesame seeds
1 large cucumber
2 celery sticks
1 medium-sized carrot
450g (1lb) cooked chicken
1 teaspoon English mustard
a pinch of sugar
1–2 tablespoons light soy sauce
2 tablespoons rice vinegar
3 tablespoons sunflower oil
1 teaspoon sesame oil

1 teaspoon finely chopped fresh ginger
2 tablespoons finely chopped spring onions, plus 2 spring onions cut into fine strips
1 tablespoon coriander leaves
2–4 red chillies, seeded and finely sliced (optional)
salt
freshly ground black pepper

1. Dry roast the sesame seeds in a small pan for 2–3 minutes until they turn golden and give off a fragrant aroma.

2. Peel the cucumber, then cut it in half lengthways, scoop out the seeds with a spoon and cut into fine diagonal slices. Finely shred the celery and carrot.

3. Cut or tear the chicken meat into fine shreds.

4. Combine the mustard, sugar, soy sauce, vinegar and sunflower and sesame oils. Add the ginger, chopped spring onions and sesame seeds. Mix well.

5. Pour half the dressing over the chicken and toss well, then check the seasoning and add salt and pepper to taste.

6. Lay the cucumber slices on a serving plate or dish, pile the chicken on top, then the celery and carrot. Drizzle with the rest of the dressing and garnish with the coriander and strips of spring onion, and the chillies if using.

Aubergine Salad

AUBERGINES, also known as eggplants, come in a range of colours and sizes, from huge fat ones to the small thin variety that the Chinese prefer. Steaming is the quickest way to cook aubergines, but you could bake or grill them instead. Here they are served with a roasted sesame sauce.

—— SERVES 4 ——

1 tablespoon sesame seeds
3 medium-sized aubergines
1 clove garlic, finely chopped
1 teaspoon finely chopped fresh
   ginger
2 tablespoons finely chopped spring
   onions

1 teaspoon sugar
1 tablespoon soy sauce
2 tablespoons rice vinegar
1 tablespoon olive oil
salt
freshly ground black pepper

1. Dry roast the sesame seeds in a small pan for 2–3 minutes until they turn golden and give off a fragrant aroma.

2. Steam the aubergines for about 10–12 minutes until soft, then leave to cool.

3. Remove the stem ends and peel. Tear the flesh lengthways in strips and chop roughly.

4. Combine the garlic, ginger, spring onions, sugar, soy sauce, vinegar, olive oil, roasted sesame seeds, salt and pepper. Pour the sauce over the aubergines and toss.

OPPOSITE Sweet and Sour Spare Ribs (page 88) served with Vegetable Fried Rice (page 118)

Prawn Salad with Bean Sprouts and Coriander

NOT CLASSICALLY Chinese, but this quick-and-easy hors-d'oeuvre is perfect on crostini for a cocktail party or with drinks before dinner. It also makes a satisfying snack in toasted pitta bread.

—— MAKES ABOUT 20 SNACKS ——

2 tablespoons mayonnaise
1 tablespoon lemon juice
1 tablespoon light soy sauce
1 teaspoon finely chopped fresh
   ginger
2 teaspoons tomato ketchup
   (optional)
a few shakes of Tabasco or chilli
   sauce

225g (8oz) cooked peeled prawns
1 carrot, coarsely grated
75g (3oz) bean sprouts
2 spring onions, finely chopped
4 tablespoons roughly chopped
   coriander
crostini
salt
freshly ground black pepper

1. Mix together the mayonnaise, lemon juice, soy sauce, ginger, tomato ketchup if using and Tabasco or chilli sauce to taste.

2. Add the prawns, grated carrot, bean sprouts, spring onions and coriander and mix gently. Check for seasoning and add salt and pepper to taste. Serve on the crostini.

OPPOSITE Singapore Noodles (page 124)

Tuna Tartare with Wonton Wafers

Do NOT BE afraid to try this recipe – it is delicious. You can serve it as a starter or on crostini at drinks parties. Instead of tuna you can use salmon. It is important to make sure the fish is absolutely fresh as it is eaten raw, although the acidity in the pickled ginger and lime juice does 'cook' it slightly. The wonton wrappers can be fried in advance, if you prefer.

—— SERVES 4 – 6 ——

450g (1lb) fresh tuna, trimmed
2 spring onions, finely sliced
1 tablespoon chopped pickled
   ginger
1 small dill-pickled gherkin, finely
   chopped
1 tablespoon chopped dill
1 teaspoon soy sauce
a few shakes of Worcestershire
   sauce
a few shakes of Tabasco

juice of 1 lime
1–2 tablespoons olive oil
115g (4oz) young salad leaves:
   lamb's lettuce or baby spinach
4 tablespoons diced mixed red,
   yellow and green peppers
   (optional)
oil for deep frying
4 wonton wrappers
salt
freshly ground black pepper

—————— ◆ ——————

1. Chop the tuna into small pieces and place in a bowl.

2. Add the spring onions, pickled ginger, gherkin and dill. Mix, then add the soy sauce, Worcestershire sauce, Tabasco, lime juice and olive oil and season with salt and pepper.

3. Divide the tuna mixture into portions and shape them into rounds, then place on individual plates and garnish with the salad leaves and the diced peppers, if using.

4. Heat the oil for deep frying in a deep fryer or wok. Halve the wonton wrappers diagonally then slide a few into the hot oil. Fry until they expand and turn golden. Remove and drain on absorbent kitchen paper. Repeat with the remaining wrappers. Serve with the tuna.

Crispy Seaweed

CRISPY SEAWEED is a popular dish in Chinese restaurants. This is both delicious and easy to make. The secret ingredient is cabbage! In fact there is no seaweed in the recipe at all. You can buy prepared cabbage, ready for the fryer, from Chinese supermarkets. I like to sprinkle mine with dried shredded pork which is also available in most Chinese supermarkets.

—— SERVES 4 – 6 ——

2 tablespoons pine kernels
1kg (2lb 2oz) green cabbage
oil for deep frying

1 teaspoon salt
1 teaspoon demerara sugar

———————— ◆ ————————

1. Dry roast the pine kernels in a small pan for 2–4 minutes until they turn golden brown.

2. Separate the stalks and stems from the leaves of the cabbage. Only the leaves are used and you can keep the stalks for things like stir-fries.

3. Wash the leaves and dry them in a salad spinner. Roll up the leaves and shred them finely.

4. Heat the oil and deep-fry the shredded leaves in batches until they turn dark green and crisp. Remove and drain well on absorbent kitchen paper. When ready to serve, sprinkle with the salt, sugar and pine kernels.

Prawn Crackers

THESE CHINESE crisps are made from a combination of prawn meat, starch and seasoning, which is pounded and dried. They are sold in Chinese supermarkets.

—— SERVES 4 – 6 ——

oil for deep frying
1 packet of prawn crackers

———— ♦ ————

1. Heat the oil: To see if it is hot enough, simply drop a piece of prawn cracker into it. The cracker should puff up and float to the top.

2. Deep-fry the crackers, a small handful at a time. Once they have puffed up, remove with a slotted spoon and drain on absorbent kitchen paper.

SOUPS

S OUP IS AN IMPORTANT part of a Chinese meal and is nearly always served.

Chinese soups are served alongside the meal, rather than as a first course, except for formal occasions and at banquets where the more complex and magnificent soups like bird's nest or shark's fin are served separately – usually towards the end of the meal.

Chinese soups are extremely varied, ranging from light to heavy, from simple to complex. In general, light soups are preferred as they are not only quick and easy to prepare, they are also delicious. Most soups are based on a beautifully light stock, which has various meats and vegetables added to it. They should never be boiled too vigorously or for too long, as they lose their flavour and clarity.

Chicken Stock

ONE OF THE essentials in any kitchen is a well-made stock. A good one makes a world of difference to soups. Make a big batch, use as much as you need and freeze the rest.

——MAKES ABOUT 3–3.5 LITRES (5–6 PINTS)——

*1.5kg (3–3½ lb) meaty chicken
  carcass
450g (1lb) pork bones (optional)
2 slices of fresh ginger
1 onion
1 leek*

*2 carrots
1 celery stick
10 crushed black peppercorns
a small handful of coriander leaves
  (optional)*

1. Place the chicken carcass and pork bones, if using, in a large pan. Add 4 litres (7 pints) of water. Bring to the boil, reduce the heat and skim off any foam that rises to the top.

2. Add the ginger slices, onion, leek, carrots, celery, peppercorns, and coriander if using. Bring to a simmer, cover the pan with a lid and simmer for 2–2½ hours.

3. Remove from the heat and strain through a fine sieve. If you don't need the stock right away, it is a good idea to leave it to cool, preferably overnight – the fat on top will congeal and it will be easy to remove it.

Monkfish and Watercress Soup

A SIMPLE, CLEAN-TASTING soup which makes an elegant start to any meal.

── SERVES 4–6 ──

225g (8oz) monkfish tail, trimmed
4 slices of fresh ginger, finely shredded
1 tablespoon rice wine or medium-
  dry sherry
1 tablespoon light soy sauce
1 teaspoon cornflour
1 teaspoon sesame oil
1 litre (1³/4 pints) chicken stock (see
  page 32) or fish stock

225g (8oz) tofu, cut into 2.5cm
  (1 inch) cubes
2 bunches of watercress, stalks
  removed
2 spring onions, chopped
1 tablespoon chopped fresh
  coriander leaves
salt
freshly ground black pepper

◆

1. Slice the fish into fine slivers and place in a bowl. Add the ginger, rice wine or sherry, soy sauce, cornflour and sesame oil. Mix gently.

2. Bring the stock to the boil. Add the tofu, watercress and spring onions and simmer for 3 minutes. Add the fish and stir to separate. Season to taste with salt and pepper.

3. Garnish with the coriander.

Velvety Chicken and Sweetcorn Soup

A VERY POPULAR and easy soup to make, but delicious nevertheless. It is well known in Chinese restaurants and takeaways. The sweet, delicate flavour of sweetcorn also goes very well with crabmeat.

—— SERVES 4–6 ——

175g (6oz) minced chicken
1 teaspoon chopped fresh ginger
1 tablespoon medium-dry sherry
1.2 litres (2 pints) chicken stock
   (see page 32)
1 × 565g (1lb 4oz) can of creamed
   or crushed sweetcorn

1 tablespoon soy sauce
2 tablespoons cornflour
2 egg whites
2 slices smoked ham, finely sliced
2 spring onions, finely chopped
salt
freshly ground black pepper

1. Place the chicken in a bowl. Season with salt and pepper, then add the ginger and sherry and mix.

2. Bring the stock to the boil. Add the chicken mixture and sweetcorn. Stir to loosen the mixture and simmer for 7–8 minutes. Add the soy sauce and season with salt and pepper.

3. Mix the cornflour to a smooth paste with a couple of spoonfuls of water. Add to the soup and stir until it thickens. Adjust the seasoning with salt and pepper.

4. Beat the egg whites with 1 tablespoon water until mixed, then slowly add in a thin stream, stirring well.

5. Garnish the soup with the smoked ham and spring onions.

Pork and Szechuan Pickle Soup

SZECHUAN PICKLES are made from kohlrabi and are yellowish-green in colour and hot and salty with a lovely crunchy texture. They are available from Chinese food stores, and come either whole or shredded in cans. They can be stir-fried with meat or fish. They should always be rinsed thoroughly, and sometimes soaked before use, because of their saltiness.

—— SERVES 4–6 ——

50g (2oz) cellophane noodles
225g (8oz) lean pork
1 tablespoon soy sauce
1 tablespoon medium-dry sherry
1 egg white
1 tablespoon cornflour
1.2 litres (2 pints) chicken stock
  (see page 32)

75g (3oz) Szechuan pickles, finely
  sliced or shredded, soaked for 5
  minutes and rinsed
2 tablespoons chopped spring
  onions
salt
freshly ground black pepper

1. Soak the cellophane noodles in warm water for 20–30 minutes, then drain and cut into short lengths.

2. Meanwhile, finely slice or shred the pork. Combine the soy sauce, sherry, egg white and cornflour. Add the pork and mix well.

3. Bring the stock to the boil. Add the pork and Szechuan pickles, then return the stock to the boil and add the noodles. Simmer for 6–7 minutes or until the noodles are tender.

4. Check for seasoning and add salt and pepper to taste. Sprinkle with the spring onions just before serving.

Short Soup

THIS IS ONE of my all-time favourite soups. Short soups are often made into long soups with the addition of noodles. Wonton wrappers are available from chilled counters in Chinese food stores. They also freeze well.

—— SERVES 4–6 ——

225g (8oz) minced chicken or pork
2 spring onions, finely chopped
4–5 canned water chestnuts,
    drained and chopped
2 tablespoons chopped canned
    bamboo shoots
1 tablespoon soy sauce, plus a little
    extra
1 teaspoon sesame oil

24 wonton wrappers
1.2 litres (2 pints) chicken stock
    (see page 32)
50g (2oz) iceberg or cos lettuce
    leaves, shredded
2 spring onions, chopped (to garnish)
salt
freshly ground black pepper

1. Combine the chicken or pork with the finely chopped spring onions, the water chestnuts and bamboo shoots. Add the soy sauce and sesame oil and season with salt and pepper.

2. Place about ¹/₂ to 1 teaspoon of the mixture in the centre of a wonton wrapper, bring the edges up over the filling and pinch to seal. Repeat with the remaining wrappers.

3. Bring a pan of water to the boil. Add the wontons and simmer until they float, about 5 minutes. Drain and keep warm.

4. Meanwhile, heat the stock to boiling point. Add the lettuce leaves and adjust the flavour with salt, pepper and soy sauce.

5. Divide the wontons among soup bowls. Pour the boiling stock over them and garnish with the chopped spring onions.

Chicken and Cucumber Soup

A LIGHT AND refreshing soup, with a delicate flavour of cucumber.

—— S ERVES 4–6 ——

1 cucumber
225g (8oz) minced chicken
1 tablespoon soy sauce
1 tablespoon medium-dry sherry
2 tablespoons cornflour
1 egg white

1.2 litres (2 pints) chicken stock
 (see page 32)
2 tablespoons finely chopped spring
 onions
salt
freshly ground black pepper

1. Peel the cucumber, slice it in half lengthways and scrape out the seeds with a spoon. Slice the halves into 2.5cm (1 inch) lengths.

2. Put the chicken, soy sauce, sherry, cornflour and egg white in a food processor and mix well.

3. Bring the stock to the boil. Form the chicken mixture into balls about the size of small walnuts. Drop the balls into the boiling stock and, when they float to the top, add the cucumber slices. Bring back to the boil, check for seasoning and add salt and pepper to taste. Garnish with the spring onions.

Tofu, Pork and Vegetable Soup

THIS SIMPLE, hearty soup uses familiar ingredients that are available in most supermarkets. The vegetables are stir-fried first in order to reduce their moisture and bring out their characteristic flavours. Cornflour is added at the end to thicken the soup and also to keep it hot longer.

—— SERVES 4–6 ——

4 fresh shiitake mushrooms
2 tablespoons sunflower oil
2 slices of fresh ginger, shredded
175g (6oz) lean pork, shredded
1 carrot, finely shredded
1 small leek, shredded
50g (2oz) canned bamboo shoots,
  rinsed, drained and shredded

1.2 litres (2 pints) chicken stock
  (see page 32)
300g (10oz) tofu, crumbled
1–2 tablespoons soy sauce
2 tablespoons cornflour
2 tablespoons coriander leaves
salt
freshly ground black pepper

——————— ◆ ———————

1. Remove the stems from the mushrooms and finely slice the caps.

2. Heat the oil in a large pan over a medium heat. Add the ginger and pork and fry until they change colour. Add the carrot, leek, mushroom caps and bamboo shoots and cook until softened. Add the stock and tofu.

3. Bring the soup to the boil, add the soy sauce and season with salt and pepper. Mix the cornflour to a paste with 3 tablespoons water and stir into the soup to thicken it. Garnish with the coriander.

Beef, Tomato and Egg-Flower Soup

THIS IS A LIGHT, summery soup. Chicken, pork or shellfish can be used instead of beef.

—— SERVES 4–6 ——

175g (6oz) lean beef
1 tablespoon chopped fresh ginger
1 tablespoon soy sauce
1 tablespoon medium-dry sherry
1 tablespoon cornflour
1 tablespoon sunflower oil
4–6 tomatoes, peeled and roughly
  chopped

1.2 litres (2 pints) chicken stock
  (see page 32)
2 eggs
4 spring onions, chopped
salt
freshly ground black pepper

1. Finely slice and then roughly chop the beef. Combine the ginger, soy sauce, sherry and cornflour. Add the beef and mix well.

2. Heat the oil in a saucepan. Add the beef and stir-fry until it changes colour. Add the tomatoes and season with salt and pepper, then add the stock and bring to the boil. Reduce the heat and leave to simmer for 5–7 minutes.

3. Beat the eggs and slowly pour them into the soup. Do not allow the soup to boil. Stir gently once – the egg will float to the top. Garnish with the spring onions and serve at once.

Spiced Chicken Soup

A LIGHT AND fragrant soup from Northern China. The original uses the region's best-known vegetable – the Tientsin cabbage. For vegetarians, omit the chicken and use vegetable stock. This recipe uses Chinese cabbage, but white or Savoy cabbage make good alternatives.

—— SERVES 4–6 ——

75g (3oz) cellophane noodles
2 tablespoons groundnut oil
1 teaspoon chopped garlic
1 onion, finely chopped
1 teaspoon five-spice powder
1 tablespoon peanut butter
1.2 litres (2 pints) chicken stock
   (see page 32)

115g (4oz) Chinese cabbage (see
   page 3), shredded
115g (4oz) bean sprouts
115g (4oz) cooked chicken, shredded
2 spring onions, chopped
salt
freshly ground black pepper

1. Soak the cellophane noodles in warm water for 20–30 minutes then drain and cut into short lengths.

2. Heat the oil in a large pan. Add the garlic, onion and five-spice powder and fry until softened.

3. Add the peanut butter and stir well. Add the chicken stock, bring to a quick boil and season with salt and pepper to taste.

4. Add the noodles and cook for 3 minutes, then add the cabbage and bean sprouts. Simmer for another 5–6 minutes.

5. Garnish with the shredded chicken and spring onions, and serve while hot.

Hot-Sour Soup

WOOD AND CLOUD ears are edible Chinese fungi that grow in large quantities on trees in the western provinces of Szechuan and Yunnan. They are eaten not so much for their flavour, but for their crunchy texture. They are sold dried and must be soaked before use.

—— SERVES 4–6 ——

2 tablespoons sunflower oil
2 cloves garlic, chopped
2 dried chillies, seeded and chopped
115g (4oz) lean pork, cut into fine
  strips
2 tablespoons wood or cloud ear
  mushrooms, soaked, trimmed and
  sliced (see page 5)
50g (2oz) canned bamboo shoots,
  rinsed, drained and shredded
1.2 litres (2 pints) chicken stock
  (see page 32)

175g (6oz) tofu, diced
1 tablespoon medium-dry sherry
2–3 tablespoons red wine vinegar,
  plus extra for serving (optional)
1 tablespoon soy sauce
2 tablespoons cornflour
1 egg, beaten
1 teaspoon sesame oil
2 spring onions, finely chopped
salt
freshly ground black pepper

1. Heat the oil in a large pan. Add the garlic, chillies, pork, wood or cloud ears and bamboo shoots and stir-fry for 2–3 minutes. Add the stock and bring to a quick boil, then turn the heat to low and simmer gently for 6–8 minutes.

2. Add the tofu, sherry, vinegar and soy sauce. Simmer for a further 5 minutes.

3. Blend the cornflour with a couple of spoonfuls of water and stir into the soup. When the soup boils and thickens, slowly pour in the egg, stirring so that it becomes strands and floats to the top.

4. Check for seasoning and add salt and pepper to taste. Sprinkle with the sesame oil and spring onions and serve at once. You can offer some red wine vinegar separately.

EGG DISHES

E GGS CAN be cooked in all possible ways. They can be steamed, stirred or scrambled, boiled or pan-fried. Their uses are numerous.

Eggs are not usually cooked alone, but are combined with other ingredients to make delicious omelettes and stirred-egg dishes. One of my all-time favourites is a simple fried egg, crisp and crusty on the outside and soft and velvety inside.

The most important thing to remember when cooking eggs is to use a low heat, unless you are making an omelette.

Always store eggs in the refrigerator, and keep them away from strong smelling foods. For best results, bring the eggs to room temperature before using them in your cooking.

Savoury Egg Custards

THESE SAVOURY custards are a favourite with young and old. They are delicately flavoured, and have a velvety consistency. In China, where dishes at a meal tend to be communal, the custard comes in a large bowl. For Western-style meals, use individual dishes like teacups or ramekins which will make servings that much easier to handle. I like to serve the custards as a starter.

—— SERVES 4 ——

75g (3oz) lean chicken meat, diced
4 tiger prawns, shelled and deveined
4 shiitake mushrooms, sliced
8–10 spinach leaves, blanched
4 tablespoons chopped spring onions
500ml (16fl oz) chicken stock (see page 32)

1 teaspoon chopped fresh ginger
1 teaspoon light soy sauce
3 large eggs
salt
freshly ground black pepper

1. Season the chicken with salt and pepper and divide among four heat-proof dishes along with the prawns, mushrooms, spinach leaves and spring onions.

2. Combine the stock with the ginger, soy sauce, eggs and salt to taste. Beat well and strain through a sieve into the dishes.

3. Cover the dishes with lids or cling film and place in a steamer. Cover the steamer and steam over high heat for 2 minutes, then lower the heat and continue steaming for 12 minutes. Alternatively, cover the cups or ramekins with foil, place in a roasting tin filled with 2.5cm (1 inch) of hot water and bake in an oven preheated to 180°C/350°F/Gas 4 for 20–25 minutes. To test whether the custard is done, insert a cocktail stick or skewer; the custard is done when it draws out clear liquid.

Golden Coin Purse Eggs with Oyster Sauce

THE NAME of these fried eggs comes from their appearance: the shape of the folded-over white looks like a purse, while the yolk inside is like a large golden coin. As a child, I used to love the crispy whites, but best of all is when you break the inside and all the lovely yolk just oozes out. Nowadays, though, we have to be careful about who we serve undercooked eggs to.

—— SERVES 4 ——

3 tablespoons sunflower oil
4 eggs
2 teaspoons soy sauce

1 tablespoon oyster sauce
4 tablespoons coriander leaves

———— ◆ ————

1. Heat the oil in a wok or large frying pan until it is almost smoking.

2. Break one egg on to a small plate or saucer, then gently slide it into the centre of the pan. As soon as the edges begin to brown slightly, flip one half of the egg over with a spatula or fish slice to form a half-moon shape.

3. Fry over a medium heat until the bottom is lightly set. Turn over and brown the other side. Remove and keep warm while you repeat the process with the remaining eggs. Sprinkle with the soy and oyster sauce. Garnish with the coriander and serve over rice or noodles.

Stir-Fried Eggs with Beef

THIS IS A quick and easy dish to throw together when you are in a hurry and feeling peckish. You can use pork, chicken, prawns or vegetables instead of beef and stir-fry as long as necessary. Served on toasted ciabatta, it makes a tasty snack.

—— SERVES 4 ——

175g (6oz) sirloin steak
1 teaspoon medium-dry sherry
1 tablespoon soy sauce
1 teaspoon chopped fresh ginger
½ teaspoon cornflour
5 large eggs

4 tablespoons finely sliced spring
   onions
4 tablespoons sunflower oil
salt
freshly ground black pepper

1. Remove any fat and gristle from the beef and slice thinly. Combine the sherry, soy sauce, ginger and cornflour. Add the beef slices and mix well.

2. Beat the eggs in a large bowl, add half the spring onions and season with a pinch of salt and pepper.

3. Heat half the oil in a wok or large frying pan until very hot, add the beef and stir with a spatula to separate the meat. Fry for 1–2 minutes or until the meat changes colour, then add the meat to the beaten eggs and mix.

4. Wipe the pan clean and heat the remaining oil until very hot, then pour in the egg and meat mixture and stir-fry until the eggs are scrambled and lightly set. Garnish with the remaining spring onions.

Stirred Eggs with Bacon and Garlic Chives

GARLIC OR Chinese chives are members of the onion family, with narrow, flat green leaves. They look like a cross between chives and spring onions, and have a pungent flavour.

—— SERVES 4 ——

3 tablespoons sunflower oil
4 slices of rindless back bacon,
  chopped
115g (4oz) garlic chives, cut into
  short lengths

4–6 eggs
salt
freshly ground black pepper

1. Heat the oil in a wok or large frying pan. Add the bacon and fry until lightly done, then add the garlic chives and stir-fry until softened.

2. Beat the eggs, season with a little salt and pepper, then add them to the bacon and chives and cook over a medium-high heat. As the eggs begin to set, draw them away from the edges of the pan and towards the centre with a fork or spatula. The eggs are best when slightly soft.

Stirred Eggs with Tomatoes

THIS IS A lovely dish in the summer when tomatoes are tasty and plentiful. It is light and very popular with children.

—— SERVES 4 ——

4 tablespoons sunflower oil
1 teaspoon chopped garlic
1 tablespoon chopped fresh ginger
450g (1lb) tomatoes, peeled and
    roughly chopped
1 teaspoon sugar

120ml (4fl oz) chicken stock or water
6 eggs
4 spring onions or a small handful
    of basil, chopped
salt
freshly ground black pepper

1. Heat half the oil in a wok or saucepan. Add the garlic and ginger and fry for 30 seconds until fragrant. Add the tomatoes and sugar and season with salt and pepper. Stir-fry for 1 minute, add the stock or water, then cover and simmer for 6–8 minutes or until the tomatoes are soft and pulpy.

2. Meanwhile, beat the eggs with a pinch of salt and pepper. Add the spring onions or basil.

3. Heat the remaining oil in a wok or large frying pan. When it is just beginning to smoke, pour in the egg mixture. As the mixture swells and begins to set, draw it away from the edges of the pan towards the centre with a fork, then turn over and brown the other side. Do not overcook.

4. Chop the cooked eggs roughly and add to the tomato sauce for just long enough for it to reheat. Adjust the seasoning and serve immediately.

Prawn and Crab Omelettes

THESE MAKE a good starter, or a light lunch with a tossed salad.

—— SERVES 4 ——

8 eggs
2 spring onions, chopped, plus 2
    spring onions, cut diagonally into
    thin slices
50g (2oz) button mushrooms, sliced
1 celery stick, chopped

225g (8oz) cooked peeled prawns
115g (4oz) white crabmeat
4 tablespoons sunflower oil
2 tablespoons coriander leaves
salt
freshly ground black pepper

Sauce

1 teaspoon sunflower oil
2 shallots, chopped
1 teaspoon chopped fresh ginger
2 teaspoons soy sauce

180ml (6fl oz) chicken stock (see
    page 32)
1 tablespoon oyster sauce
2 teaspoons cornflour

————— ◆ —————

1. Make the sauce: Heat the oil in a small saucepan. Add the shallots and ginger and fry until fragrant. Add the soy sauce, chicken stock and oyster sauce and bring to the boil. Dissolve the cornflour in 1 table-spoon of water and stir into the sauce to thicken. Keep warm.

2. Beat the eggs in a bowl and season with salt and pepper. Add the chopped spring onions, mushrooms, celery, prawns and crabmeat. Mix well.

3. Add about 1 tablespoon of oil to a small frying pan and heat. When hot, use a cup or a ladle as measure and pour in some of the egg mixture.

4. When the omelette is firm on one side, turn it over and cook the other side. Transfer to a warm plate and keep warm while you cook the remaining omelettes, stacking them on the plate. The mixture should make 10–12 small omelettes.

5. Reheat the sauce if necessary, and pour over the stack of omelettes. Garnish with the sliced spring onions and coriander.

FISH AND SEAFOOD

FISH AND SEAFOOD are ideal for cooks in a hurry as they take no time to cook and are full of goodness – high in protein and low in fat.

The Chinese like their fish to be as fresh as possible and prefer freshwater varieties. Fish is often taken home from the market in a plastic bag of water and only killed immediately prior to cooking.

In China fish is cooked in a wide variety of ways, all of them accomplished with great taste and skill. One of the best-loved methods is steaming. The fish is kept whole and is cleaned and scaled. It is placed on a shallow, heatproof dish and a sprinkling of shredded ginger is added. It is then steamed, and all the cooking juices are retained in the dish. Lastly, a drizzle of hot oil and soy sauce is added. A very simple but succulent way of cooking fish.

As for seafood, needless to say the Chinese eat everything that is available to them: oysters, scallops, crabs, abalones, shrimps, lobsters, mussels and clams are the most common. In fact, the Chinese word for shellfish translates literally as 'sea freshness'.

Seared Tuna with Chilli Sauce

TUNA, KING FISH, salmon and mackerel stand up to the chilli sauce very well. Choose small, thick steaks rather than big, thin ones as there is less risk of overcooking them – these fish tend to get very dry when overdone. As an alternative to rice, mashed potatoes and a green vegetable go very nicely with this dish.

—— SERVES 4 ——

3 tablespoons sunflower oil

4 tuna steaks, each weighing about 150g (5oz)

1 teaspoon chopped garlic

1 teaspoon chopped fresh ginger

1–2 teaspoons black bean chilli sauce, to taste

2 tomatoes, peeled, seeded and chopped

4 spring onions, finely chopped

1 tablespoon rice vinegar

1 tablespoon soy sauce

1 teaspoon sugar

1 tablespoon rice wine or medium-dry sherry

120ml (4fl oz) chicken stock (see page 32) or water

1 teaspoon cornflour

salt

freshly ground black pepper

1. Heat half the oil in a wok or large frying pan. Add the fish and fry for 1–2 minutes on both sides. The steaks must be brown on the outsides, but still pink inside. Remove the fish and set aside. Keep warm.

2. Wipe the pan clean and heat the remaining oil. Add the garlic, ginger and black bean chilli sauce and stir-fry until fragrant, about 30 seconds (take care not to get too close, or the chilli might get into your eyes and nose). Add the tomatoes, half the spring onions and the rice vinegar. Stir and cook gently for 1–2 minutes.

3. Mix together the soy sauce, sugar, rice wine or sherry, stock or water and cornflour. Stir into the tomato mixture until it boils and thickens, then cook for a further few minutes until the sauce blends together. Return the steaks and their juices to the pan for just long enough to reheat and for the sauce to coat the fish. Check for seasoning and add salt and pepper to taste. Garnish with the remaining spring onions.

Pan-Fried Fish Steaks

THIS IS another quick recipe. I like the contrast between the crispy texture on the outside and the tender, succulent flesh inside. You can serve this with a tossed salad and crispy bread, or as part of a Chinese meal with rice and vegetables.

—— SERVES 4 ——

4 firm white fish or salmon steaks
   or rainbow trout
2 tablespoons medium-dry sherry
2 cloves garlic, roughly chopped
1 tablespoon finely chopped fresh
   ginger
4 tablespoons finely sliced spring
   onions

1 tablespoon rice vinegar
3–4 tablespoons sunflower oil
1 tablespoon light soy sauce
salt
freshly ground black pepper

1. Sprinkle the fish with the sherry and garlic and season with salt and pepper. Leave for 10–15 minutes.

2. Mix the ginger, spring onions and vinegar together in a small bowl.

3. Heat the oil in a frying pan until very hot. Add the fish and brown quickly on both sides, then reduce the heat and cook until the fish is done, about 6–8 minutes depending on its thickness.

4. Top the fish with the vinegar mixture and drizzle with the soy sauce.

Batter-Fried Shark with Garlic Dipping Sauce

BATTERED FISH is loved by people of all ages. I've used lager here instead of water as it makes the lightest batter. Plaice, sole or monkfish can be used instead of shark.

—— SERVES 4 ——

1 egg
250ml (8fl oz) lager
175g (6oz) flour
1 tablespoon sesame seeds
   (optional)

oil for deep frying
675g (1½lb) shark, cut into finger-
   sized strips
2 tablespoons cornflour
salt

Garlic Dipping Sauce

1 tablespoon sunflower oil
1 tablespoon chopped fresh ginger
1 teaspoon chopped garlic
1 tablespoon brown sugar
2 tablespoons soy sauce

1 tablespoon rice vinegar
1 teaspoon cornflour
90ml (3fl oz) vegetable stock
2 tablespoons chopped spring
   onions

◆

1. Make the garlic dipping sauce: Heat the oil in a small pan, add the ginger and garlic and fry for 30 seconds until fragrant. Add the brown sugar, soy sauce and rice vinegar. Dissolve the cornflour in the stock, add to the pan and stir until the liquid boils and thickens. Add the spring onions, then remove from the heat. Keep warm.

2. In a large bowl, beat the egg with the lager, then sift in the flour and beat until smooth. Add the sesame seeds, if using.

3. Heat the oil for deep frying. Season the fish with salt and toss in the cornflour, shaking off any surplus. Working in batches, tip half the fish into the batter and stir gently to make sure the strips are coated.

4. Lift the strips of fish out of the batter and slide them into the hot oil. Fry until golden and crisp, about 3–4 minutes. Remove and drain on absorbent kitchen paper. Keep warm in a low oven and repeat with the remaining fish. Serve with the garlic dipping sauce.

Braised Mackerel with Soy Gravy

MACKEREL ARE cheap and rich in protein. Their meaty flesh lends itself particularly well to braising, and stands up to the rich soy gravy.

—— SERVES 4 ——

4 mackerel, scaled and cleaned
2 tablespoons flour
4 tablespoons sunflower oil
1 tablespoon finely chopped fresh
   ginger
1 teaspoon finely chopped garlic
4 tablespoons light soy sauce

1 teaspoon dark soy sauce
2 tablespoons rice wine or medium-
   dry sherry
2 teaspoons sugar
½ teaspoon salt
2 spring onions, chopped

1. Coat the mackerel lightly with flour and shake off any surplus.

2. Heat the oil in a wok or large frying pan until very hot. Lower in the fish and fry for 1 minute on each side to brown and seal.

3. Combine the ginger, garlic, 250ml (8fl oz) water, soy sauces, rice wine or sherry, sugar and salt and pour the mixture over the fish. Bring to a quick boil, then cover and cook over a medium heat until the fish is cooked, about 10 minutes. Turn the fish halfway through cooking. If there is a lot of liquid left in the pan, remove the fish and turn the heat high to reduce it to a sauce-like consistency. Add the spring onions and serve with plain boiled rice or small new potatoes and a green vegetable.

Steamed Fish with Chinese Mushrooms, Ginger and Spring Onions

STEAMED FISH is often finished with just a touch of soy sauce and hot oil. The topping in this recipe includes Chinese mushrooms and is one of my favourites. You can also add finely shredded pork to the mixture.

—— SERVES 4 ——

6 dried shiitake mushrooms, soaked (see page 5)

1–2 tablespoons wood ear mushrooms, soaked (see page 5)

1 tablespoon preserved cabbage, rinsed and drained (optional)

1 tablespoon finely shredded fresh ginger

4 tablespoons finely chopped spring onions

1 large whole fish, scaled and cleaned, or 4 fillets, such as sea bass, grey mullet, halibut or cod

1 tablespoon light soy sauce

1 teaspoon groundnut oil

salt

———— ◆ ————

1. Prepare the shiitake mushrooms by removing the stalks and finely slicing the caps. Finely shred the wood ears after discarding any hard, woody bits.

2. Season the mushrooms with a pinch of salt and mix them with the preserved cabbage, ginger and half the spring onions.

3. Put the fish on a plate and scatter the mushroom mixture over the top. Put the plate into a steamer, or on to a rack in a wok of simmering water. Steam for about 7–10 minutes, depending on the thickness of the fish.

4. Remove the plate of cooked fish from the steamer and sprinkle with the remaining spring onions and the soy sauce and oil.

Steamed Plaice with Sesame and Soy Dressing

ANOTHER speedy dish. This is very good with salad, spinach or stir-fried vegetables. You can use sole instead of plaice – or even trout, which will give a very pretty pink colour.

—— SERVES 4 ——

2 tablespoons sesame seeds
8–12 plaice fillets, skinned
1 tablespoon groundnut oil
2 tablespoons finely shredded fresh
  ginger
1 tablespoon chopped garlic
4 spring onions, finely chopped

2 tablespoons lime juice
1 tablespoon soy sauce
1 tablespoon oyster sauce
1 tablespoon sesame oil
salt
freshly ground black pepper

1. Dry roast the sesame seeds in a small pan for 2–3 minutes until they turn golden and give off a fragrant aroma.

2. Trim the plaice fillets and cut them lengthways down the natural dividing line. Set aside.

3. Heat the groundnut oil in a small frying pan, add the ginger and garlic and fry for about 30 seconds until fragrant. Remove from the heat and add the sesame seeds and spring onions. Mix well.

4. Season the fillets very lightly with salt and pepper. Lay them skinned side up and spread some of the sesame seed mixture over them: just use half of the mixture. Roll up the fillets firmly into neat little rolls.

5. Place the rolls on a heatproof dish and steam over simmering water for 5–6 minutes.

6. Add the lime juice, soy sauce, oyster sauce and sesame oil to the remaining sesame seed mixture and thin it down with a couple of spoonfuls of cooking juices. Spoon the dressing over the fish and serve immediately.

Sweet and Sour Grey Mullet with Cherry Tomatoes

GREY MULLET is firm-fleshed and well flavoured, a good replacement for expensive sea bass. You can also use mackerel, rainbow trout or snapper in this recipe. If you are wary of using whole fish, substitute pieces of fillet. Obviously, if you are serving this with other dishes as part of a Chinese meal, you will not need a whole fish for each person.

—— SERVES 4 ——

4 grey mullet, scaled and cleaned
2 tablespoons cornflour
120ml (4fl oz) vegetable oil
1 tablespoon chopped garlic
1 tablespoon chopped fresh ginger
1 dried chilli, seeded and chopped
2 shallots or 1 small onion, finely
  chopped
2–3 tablespoons sugar
4 tablespoons red wine vinegar

225g (8oz) cherry tomatoes
3 tablespoons tomato ketchup
1 tablespoon soy sauce
1 teaspoon cornflour
2 spring onions, cut diagonally into
  slices
2 tablespoons chopped coriander
  leaves
salt
freshly ground black pepper

1. Rinse the mullet and pat dry, then score them diagonally on both sides. Season with salt and pepper and coat thoroughly with the 2 tablespoons cornflour, shaking off any surplus.

2. Heat the oil in a wok or large frying pan. Slide the mullet into the oil and fry until crisp and brown. You may need to do this in two batches. Remove the fish with a spatula or fish slice and keep warm.

3. Pour off all but a couple of spoonfuls of the fat and heat. Add the garlic, ginger, chilli and shallots or onion and fry until fragrant and softened. Add the sugar and stir until it dissolves and takes on a light caramel colour, then add the vinegar and stir up any sediment at the bottom of the pan. Leave to bubble away for about 1 minute.

4. Add the cherry tomatoes, season with salt and pepper and cook until they start to burst. Combine the ketchup, soy sauce, 6 tablespoons of water and 1 teaspoon cornflour and pour this over the tomatoes. Stir until the mixture boils and thickens, then simmer gently for about 2–3 minutes. Adjust the seasoning.

5. Return the fish to the pan just long enough to coat with the sauce and to reheat. Garnish with spring onions and coriander, and serve with rice or potatoes.

Braised Rock Salmon with Garlic

ROCK SALMON, also known as huss or dogfish, has a meaty flesh and one central bone. It can stand up to strong flavours like garlic.

—— SERVES 4 ——

675g (1½lb) rock salmon, skinned
4 tablespoons sunflower oil
16 cloves garlic
1 teaspoon chopped fresh ginger
1 leek, finely diced
1 tablespoon rice wine or medium-
  dry sherry
2 tablespoons soy sauce

1 teaspoon sugar
1 tablespoon rice vinegar
1 teaspoon cornflour
2 red chillies, seeded and chopped
2 tablespoons chopped spring
  onions
salt
freshly ground black pepper

1. Cut the rock salmon into 3cm (1½ inch) sections.

2. Heat 2 tablespoons of the oil in a wok or large frying pan. Add the fish and fry on both sides until golden. Remove from the pan.

3. Wipe the pan clean, add 1 tablespoon of the remaining oil and reheat. Add the garlic, ginger and leek and fry until softened, about 2–3 minutes. Sit the fish neatly on top of the leek mixture.

4. Combine the rice wine or sherry, soy sauce, sugar, vinegar and 180ml (6fl oz) water. Pour this over the fish, bring to the boil, then cover and simmer for about 10 minutes. Blend the cornflour with a couple of tablespoons of water and stir into the pan to thicken the liquid. Check for seasoning and add salt and pepper to taste.

5. Heat the remaining oil and toss with the chillies and spring onions. Drizzle this mixture over the fish.

OPPOSITE Tenderloin of Lamb with Plum Sauce (page 98) served with Crisp Noodle Cake (page 121)

Steamed King Prawns with Ginger and Spring Onions

Steaming is a favourite Chinese way of cooking fish and seafood, as it ensures that all their natural juices and flavour are retained, thus preserving their delicate texture and moistness.

—— Serves 4 ——

12 large, fresh king prawns, heads
  and shells on
½ teaspoon five-spice powder
2 tablespoons rice wine or medium-
  dry sherry
1 tablespoon chopped fresh ginger

4 spring onions, chopped
1 tablespoon groundnut oil
1 tablespoon soy sauce
salt
freshly ground black pepper

1. Remove any legs from the prawns and cut the prawns in halves lengthways. Lift up the vein running along the outside curve with a cocktail stick and pull away. Rinse the prawns under running cold water, then dry them.

2. Arrange the prawns in a heatproof dish and sprinkle with a little salt and pepper and the five-spice powder, rice wine or sherry, ginger and half the spring onions.

3. Place the dish in a steamer and steam over a high heat for about 2–3 minutes. Drizzle with the oil and soy sauce. Serve at once with the remaining spring onions.

OPPOSITE Squid with Black Bean Sauce (page 65) served with simple tossed noodles and chilli sauce

Wok-Seared Scallops with Asparagus

STIR-FRYING is one of the best methods of cooking scallops as it prevents them from overcooking. You can serve these as a starter or part of a main course.

—— SERVES 4 ——

25g (1oz) pine kernels
12–16 large plump scallops with
   their coral (roe)
3 tablespoons groundnut oil
1 teaspoon chopped garlic
½ teaspoon crushed black peppercorns
450g (1lb) asparagus, cut into 3cm
   (1½ inch) lengths

120ml (4fl oz) chicken stock (see
   page 32) or water
2 teaspoons cornflour
1 tablespoon light soy sauce
1 tablespoon oyster sauce
a pinch of sugar
salt

1. Dry roast the pine kernels in a small pan for 2–4 minutes until they turn golden brown.

2. Cut the scallops in half. Cut away and discard the small crescent-shaped opaque muscle from the white flesh, and trim away any dark organs that may be attached to the orange coral. Rinse and pat dry with absorbent kitchen paper.

3. Heat half the oil in a wok or large frying pan until very hot. Add the scallops and stir-fry over a high heat for about 30–40 seconds. Remove the scallops and set them aside.

4. Heat the remaining oil in the same pan. Stir in the garlic, peppercorns and asparagus and fry for 1–2 minutes. Add the stock or water and bring to a quick boil.

5. Meanwhile, blend the cornflour, soy sauce, oyster sauce and sugar with 1 tablespoon of water. Add this to the asparagus and stir until the sauce thickens. Check for seasoning and add salt to taste.

6. Return the scallops to the pan containing the asparagus, and cook for a further minute or until the asparagus is tender. Remove from the heat, sprinkle with the roasted pine kernels and serve immediately.

Steamed Clams with Coriander

THIS IS A simple recipe that takes the minimum amount of preparation and only requires a few ingredients. You can try using mussels or oysters instead of clams.

—— SERVES 4 ——

3 tablespoons olive oil
1 onion, finely chopped
2 cloves garlic, chopped
4 dozen small, hard-shelled clams,
   cleaned

a splash of wine or water
a bunch of fresh coriander, rinsed
   and dried, stalks removed
4 tablespoons parsley leaves
2 tablespoons lemon juice

1. Heat 1 tablespoon of the oil in a large pan, then add the chopped onion and half the garlic and cook until softened.

2. Add the clams and a splash of wine or water, cover and steam for 5–7 minutes or until the clams open. Discard any that do not open.

3. Meanwhile, blend the remaining garlic and oil with the coriander leaves, parsley and lemon juice in a food processor until smooth.

4. Transfer the clams to serving bowls. Add the cooking liquid to the coriander sauce and pour this over the clams.

Stir-Fried Tiger Prawns with Cucumber

IN CHINA cucumber is used as a vegetable and more often served cooked than raw. I like pairing cucumber with prawns, as in this very pretty and fresh-looking dish.

—— SERVES 4 ——

450g (1lb) tiger prawns, shelled and
   deveined
1 tablespoon cornflour
1 cucumber
4 tablespoons sunflower oil
2 cloves garlic, crushed
2 slices of fresh ginger, shredded
1 onion, sliced

1 tablespoon brandy
115g (4oz) cherry tomatoes
4 spring onions, cut diagonally
1 tablespoon soy sauce
2 tablespoons coriander leaves
salt
freshly ground black pepper

———— ◆ ————

1. Rinse the prawns and drain them well. Season with salt and pepper, then toss them in the cornflour to coat.

2. Peel the cucumber, slice it in half lengthways and scrape out the seeds with a spoon. Cut the halves across into 5mm (¼ inch) slices.

3. Heat 2 tablespoons of the oil in a wok or large frying pan. Add the garlic and ginger and fry for 30 seconds. Add the onion and fry until it becomes translucent.

4. Add the prawns and stir-fry them until they are pink. Add the brandy and set alight to it when it is warm. When the flames have died down remove the prawns from the pan and set aside.

5. Heat the remaining oil in the same pan. Add the cucumber slices and cherry tomatoes, season with salt and pepper and stir-fry until the cucumber is translucent.

6. Return the prawns to the pan, add the spring onions and soy sauce and toss. Garnish with the coriander.

Mussels in Black Bean Sauce

Serve this in individual bowls for a wonderful starter. It also makes a great sauce for pasta. Clams can be used instead of mussels, or try a combination of both.

—— Serves 4 ——

2 tablespoons fermented black
  beans, rinsed
1 tablespoon chopped garlic
1 tablespoon chopped fresh ginger
1 teaspoon cornflour
120ml (4fl oz) light stock or water
1/2 teaspoon sugar
2 teaspoons light soy sauce
4 tablespoons sunflower oil

1–1.5kg (2–3lb) fresh mussels,
  washed and scrubbed
1 small red pepper, seeded and cut
  into small dice
2 green chillies, seeded and finely
  sliced (optional)
2 spring onions, chopped
2 tablespoons coriander leaves

1. Mash the black beans and mix them with the garlic and ginger. Blend the cornflour with the stock or water, sugar and soy sauce.

2. Heat half the oil in a wok or large frying pan until very hot. Add the mussels and stir-fry until the shells open; discard any mussels that do not open. You may need to add a splash of water. Put the mussels in a bowl and keep warm.

3. Wipe the pan clean and heat the remaining oil. Add the black bean paste and fry until fragrant. Add the diced pepper and the chillies, if using, and fry for 30 seconds.

4. Return the mussels to the pan. Stir in the stock mixture and cook until it thickens and the mussels are heated through. Garnish with the spring onions and coriander leaves.

Stir-Fried Squid with Mangetout

To make a lovely crisscross pattern on the squid, simply open the squid by cutting them lengthways. Spread them flat with the insides facing upwards. With a sharp knife make shallow, diamond-shaped cuts across the flesh. This will also help to tenderise them and make them curl up during cooking.

—— SERVES 4 ——

450g (1lb) squid tubes, cleaned
120ml (4fl oz) chicken stock (see page 32) or vegetable stock
½ teaspoon sugar
1 tablespoon soy sauce
1 tablespoon oyster sauce
1 teaspoon cornflour
4 tablespoons vegetable oil

115g (4oz) celery, sliced diagonally
115g (4oz) canned sliced bamboo shoots, rinsed and drained
4 spring onions, cut into short lengths
115g (4oz) mangetout
salt

——— ◆ ———

1. Cut the squid as described above, or into 2.5cm (1 inch) squares or into rings.

2. Combine the stock, sugar, soy sauce, oyster sauce and cornflour.

3. Heat 2 tablespoons of the oil in a wok or large frying pan until very hot. Add the squid, season with salt and stir-fry for 1 minute. Remove the squid from the pan and set aside.

4. Wipe the pan clean and heat the remaining oil. Add the celery and bamboo shoots and stir-fry for 1 minute, then add the spring onions and mangetout and stir-fry for a further minute. Pour in the stock mixture and stir until it boils and thickens.

5. Return the squid to the pan and cook until tender, about 1–2 minutes.

Squid with Black Bean Sauce

I LOVE THE taste of black beans. This recipe will work very well with prawns, chicken or beef as well as squid. Serve with rice or tossed noodles.

—— SERVES 4 ——

450g (1lb) squid, cleaned
1 tablespoon soy sauce
a pinch of sugar
1 tablespoon medium-dry sherry
1 tablespoon cornflour
1 green pepper
1 yellow pepper
1 red pepper
2 tablespoons fermented black
 beans, rinsed

2 cloves garlic, crushed
2 slices of fresh ginger
4 tablespoons vegetable oil
1 onion, sliced
120ml (4fl oz) chicken stock (see
 page 32) or vegetable stock
salt
freshly ground black pepper

1. Cut the squid into 2.5cm (1 inch) squares. Combine the soy sauce, sugar, sherry and cornflour. Add the squid and mix well.

2. Cut the peppers in half and remove the cores, seeds and ribs. Cut them into similar shapes and sizes as the squid.

3. Mash the black beans with the garlic and ginger.

4. Heat 2 tablespoons of the oil in a wok or large frying pan until very hot. Add the black bean paste and stir-fry for 30 seconds, then add the squid and stir-fry for 1 minute. Remove from the pan and set aside.

5. Wipe the pan clean and heat the remaining oil. Add the onion and peppers and stir-fry until softened, about 2 minutes. Stir in the stock and heat quickly. Return the squid to the pan, cover and cook for another 2 minutes or until tender. Check for seasoning and add salt and pepper to taste.

CHICKEN AND OTHER POULTRY

C HICKEN IS a versatile meat that can be cooked whole or in pieces, and can be stir-fried, deep-fried, steamed, simmered, braised, roasted or smoked.

Traditionally, it was a celebratory food that was served at festivals, birthdays, wedding banquets, etc. Today, we eat more chicken than ever before – it is inexpensive, low in calories and high in protein.

In general, the Chinese prefer the dark meat to the white, as they consider it to be much more tasty and succulent. The preparation times for the recipes in the following pages are minimal and the dishes need only a simple vegetable and some plain boiled rice to make a meal complete.

Duck has long been a favourite with the Chinese. It can be roasted, braised, red- or white-simmered and stir-fried. It can also be preserved with salt and dried.

Although turkey is still rare in China, I have included a few recipes in this chapter as I believe that turkey is naturally suited to Chinese cooking. It can be marinated, steamed, baked or shredded for stir-frying.

Diced Chicken with Almonds

THIS CLASSIC stir-fry combines tender pieces of chicken with the crunchy richness of almonds. Peanuts, cashew nuts, pine kernels, walnuts or even pecans can be used instead of almonds.

—— SERVES 4 ——

4 tablespoons groundnut oil
115g (4oz) whole blanched
  almonds
1 small red onion, chopped
2 cloves garlic, crushed
2 slices of fresh ginger, shredded
2 dried chillies, seeded and roughly
  chopped
450g (1lb) lean chicken, cut into
  bite-sized pieces

1 tablespoon light soy sauce
1 teaspoon dark soy sauce
1 tablespoon oyster sauce
1 teaspoon cornflour
1 teaspoon sesame oil
2 spring onions, cut diagonally into
  slices
salt
freshly ground black pepper

1. Heat the groundnut oil in a wok or large frying pan, then add the almonds and fry until golden. Remove with a slotted spoon and drain.

2. To the same pan, add the onion, garlic, ginger and chillies and fry until fragrant. Add the chicken, season with a little salt and pepper and stir-fry until it changes colour, about 3 minutes. Season with the soy and oyster sauces.

3. Combine the cornflour with 4 tablespoons water and stir into the chicken. When it thickens, mix in the sesame oil, spring onions and almonds.

Chicken with Honey, Ginger and Sweet Chilli Sauce

THIS SLIGHTLY sweet, hot and savoury chicken dish is a wonderful accompaniment to plain steamed rice or tossed noodles.

—— SERVES 4 ——

450g (1lb) chicken breasts, without
  skin
2 egg whites
2 tablespoons cornflour
oil for deep frying
2 large carrots, finely shredded into
  long strips

3 spring onions, chopped
2 tablespoons coriander leaves
2 red chillies, seeded and chopped
salt
freshly ground black pepper

Honey, Ginger and Sweet Chilli Sauce

1 tablespoon clear honey
120ml (4fl oz) chicken stock (see
  page 32) or water
juice of 1 lemon
1–2 tablespoons sweet chilli sauce
1 tablespoon soy sauce

2 teaspoons cornflour
1 tablespoon oil
2.5cm (1 inch) knob of fresh ginger,
  chopped
2 cloves garlic, chopped

1. Cut the chicken breasts into thin strips. Season with salt and pepper. Mix the egg whites and cornflour in a bowl. Add the chicken strips to the mixture and stir to coat them completely.

2. Make the sauce: Combine the honey, stock or water, lemon juice, chilli sauce, soy sauce and cornflour. Heat the oil, add the ginger and garlic, and fry until fragrant. Pour in the honey mixture and stir until the sauce boils and thickens, then simmer for 1–2 minutes. Keep warm until required.

3. Heat the oil for deep frying. First, deep-fry the carrots until they are crisp and golden. Drain on absorbent kitchen paper. Next, deep-fry the chicken strips in batches until golden brown and cooked through, about 2–3 minutes. Drain on absorbent paper. Once all the chicken strips have been cooked, toss them with the sauce and add the spring onions and fried carrots.

4. Garnish with the coriander and chillies and serve hot.

A.M.'s Hoisin Chicken

A. M. IS A 12-year-old boy and I often cater for dinner parties given by his parents. Whenever I am there, this is one of his treats. Serve with hashed brown potatoes or potato latkes.

—— SERVES 4 ——

4 chicken breasts	4 tablespoons hoisin sauce
1 tablespoon rice wine or sherry	3 tablespoons sunflower oil
1 tablespoon light soy sauce	4 tablespoons coriander leaves

1. Marinate the chicken breasts in the rice wine or sherry, soy sauce, 2 tablespoons of the hoisin sauce and 1 tablespoon of the oil for about 10 minutes.

2. Heat the remaining oil in a frying pan until hot, then add the chicken breasts and fry for about 3–4 minutes on each side or until they are cooked, turning once or twice. You can also grill or barbecue the chicken.

3. Remove the chicken breasts and brush the tops with the remaining hoisin sauce. Deglaze the pan by adding a couple of tablespoons of water and stirring to scrape up and dissolve any sediment or juices at the of the bottom of the pan. Spoon the liquid over the chicken. Garnish with the coriander.

Deep-Fried Chicken

CHINESE-STYLE fried chicken. The secret is allowing the marinade enough time to steep into the meat and develop its flavour, so it's best to marinate the chicken the night before, or in the morning. You can serve this hot or cold with cucumber or vegetable pickles. Instead of buying a whole chicken, you can use just drumsticks or wings.

—— SERVES 4 ——

1 medium-sized chicken, cut into
  8–10 joints
2 cloves garlic, crushed
2 tablespoons ground ginger
2 tablespoons chopped spring
  onions
3 tablespoons light soy sauce
2 tablespoons medium-dry sherry
juice of 1 lemon

a pinch of sugar
1 egg, beaten
oil for deep frying
4–5 tablespoons cornflour
4–6 sprigs of coriander
1 lemon, cut into quarters
salt
freshly ground black pepper

1. Place the chicken joints in a bowl, season with a little salt and pepper, then add the garlic, ginger, spring onions, soy sauce, sherry, lemon juice and sugar. Mix well and leave to marinate for as long as you can.

2. Remove the chicken joints from the bowl and drain well. Discard the marinade and return the joints to the bowl. Stir in the beaten egg and mix well.

3. Heat the oil. Dredge the chicken joints in the cornflour, shaking off any surplus. Deep-fry a few joints at a time for about 6–7 minutes, or until they are cooked and golden. Drain on absorbent kitchen paper and keep warm in a low oven until all the chicken is cooked.

4. Garnish with the coriander and lemon quarters.

Braised Chicken Wings with Black Bean Sauce

CHICKEN WINGS are cheap and often overlooked in the West. The Chinese love them for their texture and the lovely sauce that they are cooked in.

—— SERVES 4 ——

12–15 chicken wings
2 cloves garlic, crushed
2 tablespoons fermented black
    beans, rinsed
1 tablespoon oil
1 teaspoon sugar
250ml (8fl oz) chicken stock (see
    page 32) or water

1 green pepper, seeded and diced
2 spring onions, chopped
1 tablespoon soy sauce
1 tablespoon cornflour
salt
freshly ground black pepper

————— ✦ —————

1. Cut the chicken wings into sections.

2. Mash the garlic with the black beans.

3. Heat the oil in a wok or large frying pan. Add the black bean paste and stir-fry for 30 seconds. Add the chicken sections and brown lightly. Season with a pinch of salt, pepper and the sugar.

4. Stir in the stock or water and bring to the boil. Cover and simmer for 10 minutes. Add the green pepper, spring onions and soy sauce and cook for another 5–6 minutes.

5. Blend the cornflour to a paste with 1 tablespoon water and stir this into the sauce to thicken. Cook for a further 1–2 minutes.

Stir-Fried Chicken with Brown Bean Sauce

CHICKEN IS A very versatile meat that can be prepared in many different ways – its distinctive but mild flavour blends well with seasonings, herbs and spices.

—— SERVES 4 ——

450g (1lb) chicken breasts
6 dried shiitake mushrooms, soaked
   and trimmed (see page 5)
1 green pepper, seeded
150g (25oz) canned bamboo shoots,
   rinsed and drained
1 teaspoon cornflour
½ teaspoon sugar
1 tablespoon light soy sauce
1 tablespoon medium-dry sherry
120ml (4fl oz) chicken stock (see
   page 32) or water

2 tablespoons groundnut oil
2 cloves garlic, crushed
1 tablespoon shredded fresh ginger
1 tablespoon brown bean paste or
   sauce
1 teaspoon dark soy sauce
2 spring onions, cut into short
   lengths
1 teaspoon chilli oil (optional)
2 tablespoons coriander leaves
salt
freshly ground black pepper

1. Cut the chicken into 2.5cm (1 inch) cubes. Cut the mushrooms into quarters. Cut the pepper into similar sizes. Slice the bamboo shoots, if necessary, into similar sizes.

2. Blend the cornflour, sugar, light soy sauce, sherry and stock or water to a paste.

3. Heat the oil in a wok or large frying pan. Add the garlic and ginger and stir-fry for 30 seconds, then add the chicken and mushrooms. Stir well and cook over a high heat for about 5 minutes. Add the brown bean paste or sauce and dark soy sauce and mix well. Add the peppers and bamboo shoots and continue to cook for 1–2 minutes.

4. Add the cornflour and stock mixture and stir until it boils and thickens. Check for seasoning and add salt and pepper to taste. Add the spring onions and sprinkle with the chilli oil, if using. Garnish with the coriander.

Red or Soy Chicken

You CAN cook a whole chicken, duck, poussin, quail or pigeon this way – just adjust the cooking time accordingly. The dish tastes best at room temperature. Remove the fat from any sauce that is not served with the chicken and keep it in a jar in the refrigerator. It can be used again and again as a master sauce or as a seasoning in stir-fries.

—— SERVES 4 ——

2 spring onions, cut into short
  lengths
2 cloves garlic, crushed
2 slices of fresh ginger
star anise (optional)

2 tablespoons brown sugar
120ml (4fl oz) soy sauce
6 tablespoons medium-dry sherry
4 chicken legs
a small handful of coriander leaves

1. Place the spring onions in a heavy pan, along with the garlic, ginger, star anise if using, sugar, soy sauce, sherry and 120ml (4fl oz) water. Bring to the boil over a medium heat.

2. Slide in the chicken legs. Bring to the boil again, then reduce the heat, cover and simmer for about 20 minutes or until done, turning once or twice for even colouring.

3. Garnish with the coriander and serve hot or cold with the sauce.

White Chicken with Ginger and Spring Onion Dipping Sauce

THIS IS based on a classic Cantonese chicken dish, where usually the whole bird simmers in the gentlest heat for about half an hour, the heat is then turned off and the chicken is left to steep in the liquid as it cools. The most moist and flavoursome chicken is the result.

—— SERVES 4 ——

1.2 litres (2 pints) chicken stock (see page 32)
2 slices of fresh ginger

2 spring onions
4 free-range chicken breasts

Ginger and Spring Onion Dipping Sauce

4 tablespoons groundnut oil
1 tablespoon finely chopped fresh ginger

4 tablespoons finely chopped spring onions
1 teaspoon salt

———— ◆ ————

1. Bring the stock to the boil with the ginger slices and spring onions.

2. Add the chicken breasts and leave to simmer for 5 minutes. Turn the heat off, cover the pan and leave for another 10–15 minutes.

3. Meanwhile, make the sauce: Heat the oil in a small pan, then remove it from the heat and add the ginger, spring onions and salt. Stir well.

4. Take the chicken out of the pan and drain. Remove excess fat from the stock and reheat. Cut the chicken into bite-sized pieces and serve with the dipping sauce, a bowl of broth and some plain boiled rice.

Chicken Livers with Bamboo Shoots and Mangetout

CHICKEN LIVERS are cheap and nutritious. Make sure they are fresh when you buy them and remove any green bits. I like to cook them so that they are still pink inside, and serve them with rice or pasta.

—— SERVES 4 ——

1 tablespoon light soy sauce
1 tablespoon medium-dry sherry
2 teaspoons cornflour
450g (1lb) chicken livers
3 tablespoons sunflower oil
2 cloves garlic, crushed
2 slices of fresh ginger, shredded
1 × 225g (8oz) can sliced bamboo
   shoots, rinsed and drained

115g (4oz) mangetout, trimmed
6 tablespoons chicken stock (see
   page 32) or water
1 tablespoon oyster sauce
a pinch of sugar
2 spring onions, cut diagonally into
   slices
salt
freshly ground black pepper

1. Combine the soy sauce, sherry and 1 teaspoon of the cornflour. Add the chicken livers and mix well.

2. Heat 1½ tablespoons of the oil in a wok or large frying pan, add the garlic and ginger and fry for 30 seconds. Add the bamboo shoots and mangetout and stir-fry to soften them slightly. Remove from the pan.

3. Heat the remaining oil in the same pan. Add the chicken livers and stir-fry over a high heat until they are nearly cooked, about 2–3 minutes.

4. Mix the remaining cornflour to a paste with the stock or water, oyster sauce and sugar.

5. Return the mangetout mixture to the livers and stir in the cornflour paste to thicken the juices. Check for seasoning and add salt and pepper to taste. Garnish with the spring onions.

Stir-Fried Turkey with Asparagus and Sugar Snap Peas

Turkeys are sold all year round these days, and you no longer have to buy a whole bird. You can use dark or white meat for this recipe – whichever you choose, turkey cooked this way is succulent and tasty. Chicken or pork can be substituted. Serve with rice or noodles.

—— Serves 4 ——

450g (1lb) turkey meat
1 teaspoon chopped garlic
1 teaspoon chopped fresh ginger
1 tablespoon rice wine or medium-dry sherry
2 tablespoons light soy sauce
3 teaspoons cornflour
120ml (4fl oz) chicken stock (see page 32)
2 tablespoons oyster sauce

a pinch of sugar
1 teaspoon sesame oil
4 tablespoons sunflower oil
1 bunch of asparagus, cut into short lengths
175g (6oz) sugar snap peas
2 spring onions, chopped
salt
freshly ground black pepper

1. Slice the turkey meat into thin slivers. Place in a bowl with the garlic, ginger, rice wine or sherry, 1 tablespoon of the soy sauce and 2 teaspoons of the cornflour, and mix well.

2. Stir together the stock, oyster sauce, sugar, sesame oil and the remaining soy sauce and cornflour.

3. Heat 2 tablespoons of the sunflower oil in a wok or large frying pan until very hot. Add the turkey slices and stir-fry until the meat separates and loses its pink colour. Remove from the pan and set aside.

4. Wipe the pan clean and heat the remaining oil. Add the asparagus and sugar snap peas and stir-fry for about 2 minutes. Pour in the sauce mixture and stir until it boils and thickens.

5. Return the cooked turkey to the pan, toss lightly and allow to reheat. Check for seasoning and add salt and pepper to taste. Finally add the spring onions.

Scallopini of Turkey with Lemon Sauce

THIS SHARP, fresh-flavoured dish is usually associated with chicken. I have adapted it slightly for turkey.

—— SERVES 4 ——

4 large or 8 small turkey escalopes
   or steaks
2 egg whites
2 tablespoons cornflour
4–5 tablespoons sunflower oil

2 spring onions, chopped
2 red chillies, seeded and chopped
   (optional)
salt
freshly ground black pepper

Lemon Sauce

grated zest of 1 lemon
juice of 2 lemons
120ml (4fl oz) chicken stock (see
   page 32)
1 tablespoon rice wine or medium-
   dry sherry
1 tablespoon light soy sauce

1 tablespoon honey
1 tablespoon sugar
2 teaspoons cornflour
1 tablespoon sunflower oil
1 tablespoon finely chopped garlic
1 tablespoon finely chopped ginger

———— ◆ ————

1. Pound the turkey escalopes or steaks out lightly and season with salt and pepper. Mix the egg whites and cornflour, then put the turkey in the mixture and leave for 10 minutes.

2. Meanwhile, make the lemon sauce: Combine the lemon zest, lemon juice, stock, rice wine or sherry, soy sauce, honey, sugar and cornflour. Heat the oil in a small pan, then add the garlic and ginger and stir-fry until fragrant. Add the lemon mixture and stir over a low heat until it boils and thickens. Check for seasoning and add salt and pepper if necessary. Keep warm.

3. Heat the 4–5 tablespoons of oil in a large frying pan until very hot. Add the turkey and shallow-fry on both sides until cooked and lightly golden brown. Drain.

4. Serve the escalopes or steaks whole or cut into pieces. Spoon the sauce over them and garnish with the spring onions and the red chillies, if using.

Red Simmered Duck Breasts

THIS GETS its name from the rich, red-brown gravy produced by the soy sauce. The method is usually used for whole poultry or large cuts of meat and calls for slow cooking.

—— SERVES 4 ——

4 duck breasts
2 spring onions
4 slices of fresh ginger
½ star anise
6–8 Szechuan peppercorns
4 tablespoons light soy sauce

1 tablespoon dark soy sauce or
    mushroom soy sauce
4 tablespoons rice wine or medium-
    dry sherry
2 tablespoons sugar

1. Score the duck skins in crisscross fashion with a sharp knife. Place the duck breasts skin-sides down in a hot frying pan and fry gently for about 4–5 minutes to render down their fat. Turn them over to seal the other sides. Remove the breasts from the pan, rinse them quickly in hot water and pat dry.

2. Transfer the breasts to another pan, and add the remaining ingredients with water to cover. Bring to a quick simmer, cover and cook for about 6–8 minutes or until the duck is done to your liking. Turn the breasts over once or twice during cooking.

3. Remove the duck from the pan. You may want to reduce or thicken the gravy. Skim off any excess fat and serve with tossed noodles, wilted spinach or green cabbage.

Stir-Fried Duck with Green Beans

ANOTHER QUICK and tasty dish, full of flavour and texture. You can remove some or all of the duck skin. Serve with plain rice.

—— SERVES 4 ——

2 large duck breasts
1 tablespoon soy sauce
1 tablespoon medium-dry sherry
1 tablespoon cornflour
2 cloves garlic, chopped
2.5cm (1 inch) knob of fresh ginger, shredded
1 tablespoon fermented black beans, rinsed
a pinch of sugar
2 tablespoons sunflower oil
2 dried red chillies, roughly chopped

225g (8oz) fine green beans, trimmed
115g (4oz) canned water chestnuts, drained
5–6 tablespoons chicken stock (see page 32) or water
2 tablespoons oyster sauce
4 spring onions, cut diagonally into thin slices
2 large fresh red chillies, seeded and finely sliced
freshly ground black pepper

—— ◆ ——

1. Cut the duck breasts against the grain into fine slices. Combine the soy sauce, sherry and cornflour, then add the duck and mix well.

2. Mash together the garlic, ginger and black beans with the sugar.

3. Heat 1 tablespoon of the oil in a wok or large frying pan. Add the duck slices and stir-fry until they change colour, about 2–3 minutes. Remove from the pan and set aside.

4. Heat the remaining oil in the same pan. Add the dried chillies and black bean mixture and stir-fry for about 30 seconds. Add the green beans and water chestnuts and mix well. Stir in the stock or water, cover and cook for 3–4 minutes or until the beans are tender but still crisp.

5. Return the duck slices to the pan and cook for another 2–3 minutes. Season with the oyster sauce and pepper.

6. Garnish with the spring onions and fresh chillies.

Crisp-Skinned Duck Breasts with Plum Sauce

THIS PLUM sauce uses canned plums and is quick and easy to prepare. You can add some chilli if you like a sauce with a kick.

—— SERVES 4 ——

4 duck breasts
$\frac{1}{2}$ teaspoon five-spice powder
1 × 675g (1lb 8oz) can whole
   plums in natural juice, drained
   and stoned
1 teaspoon chopped fresh ginger

50g (2oz) sugar
1–2 tablespoons rice vinegar
1 teaspoon cornflour
4 spring onion tassels (optional, see
   opposite)
salt

1. Score the duck skins in crisscross fashion with a sharp knife. Season with salt and rub with the five-spice powder.

2. Place the duck breasts skin-sides down in a hot frying pan and fry gently for about 6–7 minutes so that their fat renders down and the skins become crisp. Drain off excess fat. Turn the duck breasts over to brown on the other sides and cook until they are done to your liking. Drain on absorbent kitchen paper.

3. Meanwhile, combine the plums, ginger, sugar and vinegar with 4 tablespoons water in a small pan. Stir over heat and simmer for 10–15 minutes.

4. Mix the cornflour to a paste with 1 tablespoon water and stir into the plum mixture until the sauce thickens.

5. Slice the duck and garnish with the spring onion tassels, if liked. Serve with the plum sauce.

Spring Onion Tassels

1. Wash and dry the spring onions. Trim away the roots, then trim the stalk end so that you are left with a 7.5cm (3 inch) length.

2. Make several 5cm (2 inch) long cuts through the stalk end.

3. Place in iced water and leave until the cut stalks curl up and 'bloom'.

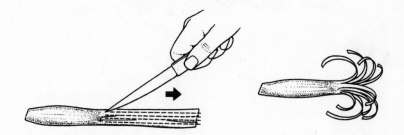

PORK, BEEF AND LAMB

W HEN IT COMES to red meat, the Chinese are ingeniously thrifty. They use every part of the animal.

Pork is the prime meat in China. Lamb is the favourite meat of the north and north-western Chinese – no doubt due to the Mongol invasion and their establishment of the Yuan dynasty from 1279–1368 – but elsewhere, lamb and mutton are rarely eaten. Because of the scarcity of cattle in China, beef cookery was never developed as fully as that of pork. However, the Chinese adapted their pork recipes to beef with ingenuity. Lamb and beef are similar in that they each have a distinctive flavour. The meats in most of the recipes that follow are interchangeable.

The Chinese way of treating meat is ideal for quick cooking as the meat is usually cut into small, thin slices of uniform size. These are very often marinated with soy sauce, fresh ginger and rice wine before being stir-fried in hot oil over an intense heat for a minimum length of time.

Shredded Pork with Bean Sprouts and Garlic Chives

THE PAIRING of bean sprouts and garlic chives is another Chinese favourite. The fresh and crunchy texture of the sprouts lends itself beautifully to the more pungent flavour of the chives.

—— SERVES 4 ——

350g (12oz) lean pork
1 egg
2 tablespoons rice wine or medium-dry sherry
1 tablespoon soy sauce
a pinch of sugar
2 teaspoons cornflour
115g (4oz) shiitake mushrooms
3–4 tablespoons groundnut oil
1–2 dried chillies (optional)

2 cloves garlic, finely chopped
1 tablespoon of fresh ginger, shredded
225g (8oz) bean sprouts
50g (2oz) garlic chives, cut into short lengths
1 teaspoon sesame oil
2 tablespoons roasted unsalted peanuts
salt
freshly ground black pepper

1. Cut the pork into fine shreds and place in a shallow dish. Beat the egg with 1 tablespoon of the rice wine or sherry, soy sauce, sugar, salt, pepper and cornflour. Pour this mixture over the pork and leave to marinate.

2. Remove the stems from the mushrooms and finely slice the caps.

3. Heat the groundnut oil in a wok or large frying pan. When it starts to smoke, stir in the dried chillies, if using, pork, garlic and ginger, toss and stir-fry over a high heat for about 5 minutes. Add the mushrooms, bean sprouts and garlic chives – you may need to add a few drops of water. Cover and cook until the bean sprouts are tender but still crisp. Adjust the seasoning and add the remaining rice wine or sherry, and the sesame oil and peanuts.

Stir-Fried Pork with Cellophane Noodles

Made from mung beans, cellophane noodles are also called bean thread, transparent, glass or pea starch noodles. They have a smooth slippery texture that readily absorbs other flavourings. They are often added to soup and can be combined with most meats and vegetables.

—— Serves 4 ——

115g (4oz) cellophane noodles
4–6 dried shiitake mushrooms,
  rinsed (see page 5)
300g (10oz) lean pork
1 tablespoon cornflour
2 tablespoons soy sauce
1 tablespoon medium-dry sherry
4 celery sticks
3 tablespoons sunflower oil

2 cloves garlic, chopped
1 tablespoon chopped fresh ginger
a pinch of sugar
250ml (8fl oz) chicken stock (see
  page 32)
1 teaspoon sesame oil
4 spring onions, chopped
salt
freshly ground black pepper

1. Soak the cellophane noodles and the shiitake mushrooms separately in warm water for 20–30 minutes.

2. Meanwhile, slice the pork into fine strips. Combine the cornflour, soy sauce and sherry, then add the pork and mix well.

3. Finely shred the celery sticks at an angle.

4. Drain the mushrooms and cellophane noodles. Finely slice the mushrooms, discarding the stalks, and cut the noodles into 5cm (2 inch) lengths.

5. Heat the sunflower oil in a wok or large frying pan. Add the garlic and ginger and stir-fry for about 30 seconds or until fragrant. Add the pork and mushrooms and stir-fry for about 2–3 minutes, then add the celery. Toss and season with the sugar and a little salt and pepper. Stir

in the stock, bring to the boil and add the noodles. Cover and cook for about 5–7 minutes or until the noodles are tender, adding more stock when necessary.

6. Remove the lid and taste for seasoning. Stir in the sesame oil and spring onions.

Pork Loin Steaks with Plum Sauce

THE SUBTLE flavour of pork complements many sauces. I serve this with mashed potatoes to soak up all that lovely plum sauce.

—— SERVES 4 ——

4 pork loin steaks
1 tablespoon cornflour
2 tablespoons rice wine or medium-dry sherry
1 tablespoon light soy sauce, plus 2 teaspoons

1 tablespoon hoisin sauce
1 teaspoon sesame oil
1 tablespoon sunflower oil
4 tablespoons plum sauce
8–10 sprigs fresh coriander

————— ◆ —————

1. Rub the pork steaks with the cornflour, rice wine or sherry, the 1 tablespoon soy sauce, and the hoisin sauce and sesame oil.

2. Heat the sunflower oil in a frying pan. Drain the pork steaks and reserve any excess marinade. Add the pork to the pan and fry on one side until brown, then fry the other side until the meat is cooked through. Remove the pork from the pan, set aside and keep warm.

3. Drain off and discard excess fat from the pan. Deglaze the pan by adding 120ml (4fl oz) water and stirring to dislodge any sediment and juices at the bottom of the pan. Add the plum sauce, the 2 teaspoons soy sauce and any marinade. Stir until the mixture boils and thickens, then reduce the heat, return the pork to the pan and cook for a few minutes until the pork steaks are coated with the sauce. Garnish with the coriander.

Sweet and Sour Spare Ribs

A CLASSIC Cantonese import, this is a favourite with many Westerners in Chinese restaurants and takeaways. Instead of pork ribs, you can use chicken, prawns or fish.

—— SERVES 4 ——

675g (1½lb) pork spare ribs or boneless shoulder of pork
2 tablespoons rice wine or medium-dry sherry
2 tablespoons soy sauce
2 cloves garlic, crushed, plus 2 cloves garlic, chopped
2 slices of fresh ginger, crushed, plus 1 teaspoon chopped fresh ginger
a pinch of sugar, plus 2 tablespoons
1 egg
oil for deep frying, plus 2 tablespoons

1 small can pineapple chunks in syrup
2 tablespoons tomato ketchup
2–3 tablespoons rice vinegar
4–6 tablespoons cornflour
2 dried chillies (optional)
1 green pepper, seeded and cut into cubes
2 spring onions, cut diagonally into slices
2 tablespoons coriander leaves
salt
freshly ground black pepper

1. Cut the ribs into about 3cm (1½ inch) lengths. Season lightly with salt and pepper and add the rice wine or sherry, soy sauce, crushed garlic, crushed ginger, the pinch of sugar and the egg. Mix well and leave to marinate. You can do this in the morning or the night before.

2. Heat the oil for deep frying. Meanwhile, drain the pineapple chunks and set aside. Reserve the syrup and mix it with the tomato ketchup, remaining sugar, vinegar and 1 teaspoon of the cornflour.

3. Dredge the ribs with the remaining cornflour, coating each piece thoroughly. Deep-fry in batches until the ribs are crisp and golden, about 6–7 minutes. Stir to separate from time to time. Drain each batch on absorbent kitchen paper and keep warm in a low oven until all the ribs are done.

4. Heat the 2 tablespoons oil in a large frying pan or wok. Add the chopped garlic, chopped ginger and dried chillies, if using, and fry for 30 seconds. Add the pepper and stir-fry for about 1 minute. Add the pineapple syrup mixture to the pan, stir until the sauce thickens and cook gently for about 4–5 minutes. Check for seasoning and add salt and pepper to taste.

5. Add the pineapple chunks and ribs to the sauce. Stir to mix and garnish with the spring onions and coriander.

Braised Pork Chops

I LIKE TO serve these rich and savoury chops with pickled salted vegetables like mustard greens pickles or Szechuan pickles. You might be surprised that hardboiled eggs are cooked in the sauce. They take on the deep colour of the sauce and actually change in texture. I do hope you will try this recipe.

—— SERVES 4 ——

4 pork chops

2 tablespoons flour

2 tablespoons sunflower oil

2 cloves garlic, crushed

50g (2oz) shallots, sliced

2 tablespoons rice wine, sake or
   medium-dry sherry

3 tablespoons light soy sauce

2 tablespoons mushroom soy sauce

1 tablespoon sugar

½ star anise

1 piece of cassia bark

4 hardboiled eggs

2 spring onions, chopped

1. Pound the pork chops with the handle of a chopping knife to flatten and tenderise them. Coat with the flour, shaking off any surplus.

2. Heat 1 tablespoon of the oil in a wok or large frying pan. Fry the chops on both sides until lightly coloured. Remove and set aside.

3. Heat the remaining oil in the same pan, add the garlic and shallots and cook until softened. Stir the rice wine, sake or sherry, light and mushroom soy sauces, sugar, star anise, cassia bark and 400ml (14fl oz) water into the pan and bring to a quick boil, then return the chops to the pan and add the eggs. Cover and simmer slowly for about 20 minutes or until the chops are tender and the liquid has reduced to a sauce. Garnish with the chopped spring onions.

OPPOSITE Sweet and Sour Grey Mullet with Cherry Tomatoes (page 56)

Stir-Fried Beef with Sweet Peppers and Oyster Sauce

A SIMPLE STIR-FRY. You can use any vegetables like mangetout, baby sweetcorn, bean sprouts etc. Another of my favourites is to add rinsed, mashed fermented black beans with the ginger and garlic.

—— S ERVES 4 ——

450g (1lb) sirloin steak, trimmed
1 tablespoon cornflour
1 teaspoon sugar
2 tablespoons light soy sauce
1 tablespoon rice wine or medium-
   dry sherry
2 tablespoons sunflower oil
1 teaspoon chopped fresh ginger

1 teaspoon chopped garlic
1 red pepper, seeded and sliced
1 yellow pepper, seeded and sliced
a bunch of spring onions, cut into
   short lengths
2–3 tablespoons oyster sauce
1 teaspoon sesame oil

1. Trim the sirloin, slice it into fine strips and place in a bowl. Add the cornflour, sugar, soy sauce and rice wine or sherry. Mix well and leave to marinate for about 10 minutes.

2. Heat the sunflower oil in a wok or large frying pan until very hot. Add the ginger and garlic and fry until fragrant. Add the sirloin strips and stir-fry for 2 minutes.

3. Add the peppers and spring onions and stir-fry for a further 2–3 minutes – you may need to add a splash of water. Lastly, add the oyster sauce and sesame oil and mix well.

OPPOSITE Firecracker Butterflied Prawns (page 21)

Sherried Beef with Chinese Greens

ANOTHER QUICK and easy dish. Most Chinese greens like *bok choy*, *choy sum* or Chinese broccoli can be used. If these are unavailable, substitute regular broccoli or spinach.

—— SERVES 4 ——

450g (1lb) fillet or sirloin steak
2 tablespoons soy sauce
2 tablespoons medium-dry sherry
1 teaspoon sugar
1 teaspoon sesame oil
450g (1lb) Chinese greens
4 tablespoons groundnut oil

2 cloves garlic, crushed
2.5cm (1 inch) knob of fresh ginger, finely shredded
½ teaspoon cornflour
6 tablespoons chicken stock (see page 32)
1 tablespoon oyster sauce

1. Cut the steak into thin slices and place in a bowl. Add the soy sauce, sherry, sugar and sesame oil and mix well.

2. Cut the Chinese greens into 5cm (2 inch) lengths, separating the leaves from the stalks.

3. Heat 2 tablespoons of the groundnut oil in a wok or large frying pan until very hot. Add the garlic and ginger and stir-fry for 30 seconds. Add the steak slices and fry for about 2 minutes or until they change colour. Remove from the pan and set aside.

4. Heat the remaining oil in the same pan. Add the stalk parts of the greens and toss and fry for 2 minutes, then add the leaves and return the steak to the pan. Mix the cornflour with the stock and oyster sauce, add to the pan and stir until the liquid boils and thickens. Serve with rice or noodles.

Satay Beef

You CAN, OF course, use lamb, pork, chicken or king prawns. Served with greens and boiled rice, this makes a truly scrumptious meal.

—— SERVES 4 ——

450g (1lb) fillet or sirloin steak in
  one piece, trimmed
2 tablespoons soy sauce
1 teaspoon sesame oil
1 tablespoon cornflour
3 tablespoons sunflower oil
2 cloves garlic, chopped
1 teaspoon curry powder

3 onions, roughly diced
3–4 tablespoons satay sauce
1 tablespoon medium-dry sherry
a large pinch of sugar
2 spring onions, cut diagonally into
  slices
salt
freshly ground black pepper

1. Cut the steak into 5mm (¼ inch) slices. Gently pound each slice to flatten it slightly. Add 1 tablespoon of the soy sauce, the sesame oil, 2 tablespoons water and the cornflour and mix well.

2. Heat 2 tablespoons of the sunflower oil in a wok or large frying pan. Add the steak slices and fry on both sides until brown, separating each slice as it goes into the pan. Remove from the pan and set aside.

3. Heat the remaining oil in the same pan. Add the garlic, curry powder and onions and stir-fry until the onions are transparent. Stir well to stop the bottom from catching.

4. Combine the satay sauce, sherry, sugar and remaining soy sauce with 2 tablespoons water. Add to the onions and stir until boiling. Return the steak slices with their juices to the pan and reheat. Check for seasoning and add salt and pepper to taste. Garnish with the spring onions and serve immediately.

Sizzling Steak

THIS IS A popular dish and fun to serve. Just be careful not to burn yourself or get splattered. You can find sizzling dishes in most general stores; they come with a cast-iron plate, wooden base and a cast-iron handle for lifting.

—— SERVES 4 ——

450g (1lb) fillet steak
4 tablespoons sunflower oil
3 onions, quartered
4 tablespoons Worcestershire sauce

6 tablespoons tomato ketchup
1 tablespoon sugar
1 tablespoon white wine or brandy

1. Put the cast-iron plate into a hot oven (220°C/425°F/Gas 7) to heat, about 15 minutes – the plate must be very hot.

2. Slice the steak thinly and flatten the slices with a meat mallet if necessary.

3. Heat 2 tablespoons of the oil in a wok or large frying pan. Add the onions and stir-fry quickly until golden brown and crisp. Remove from the pan.

4. Heat the remaining oil in the same pan. Add the steak slices and fry for 1–2 minutes over a high heat until well browned. Combine the Worcestershire sauce, tomato ketchup and sugar and mix into the steak. Stir until the sauce boils. Reduce the heat and simmer for a minute or so.

5. Remove the cast-iron plate from the oven with the handle and place it on its wooden base. Arrange the onions on the plate and spoon the steak slices over the top. Pour the wine or brandy over the plate to give the sizzling effect and serve immediately.

Stir-Fried Beef with Cauliflower

Wʜᴇɴ ᴄʜᴏᴏsɪɴɢ oyster sauce make sure you buy a good one – it will usually have the word 'superior' on its label. Cheap oyster sauce can taste metallic and fishy, whereas superior brands are velvety with a lovely savoury flavour that will enhance what you are cooking.

—— Sᴇʀᴠᴇs 4 ——

350g (12oz) lean beef
sugar
2 teaspoons soy sauce, plus
   1 tablespoon
3 teaspoons cornflour
1 small cauliflower
3 tablespoons sunflower oil

4 spring onions, chopped
120ml (4fl oz) chicken stock (see
   page 32)
2 tablespoons oyster sauce
1 tablespoon medium-dry sherry
salt
freshly ground black pepper

—— ♦ ——

1. Slice the beef thinly against the grain and mix well with a pinch of sugar, salt, pepper, 2 teaspoons of soy sauce and 1 teaspoon of the cornflour.

2. Break the cauliflower into small florets and cut the stalks diagonally into small pieces.

3. Heat 1½ tablespoons of the oil in a wok or large frying pan. Add the spring onions and beef slices and stir-fry until the beef begins to brown. Remove from the pan and set aside.

4. Heat the remaining oil in the same pan and add the cauliflower. Season with salt and a pinch of sugar and stir-fry for 1 minute. Stir in the stock and heat quickly, then cover and cook for about 5–6 minutes or until the cauliflower is tender.

5. Blend the remaining cornflour, the 1 tablespoon soy sauce and the oyster sauce and sherry with a little water.

6. Return the beef slices to the pan briefly to reheat. Stir in the cornflour paste to thicken the liquid, adjust the seasoning and serve immediately.

Stir-Fried Lamb with Ginger and Spring Onions

MUTTON AND lamb are rarely eaten except in Northern China where they are very popular, due, no doubt, to the Mongolian influence. Serve with rice or noodles.

—— SERVES 4 ——

450g (1lb) lean neck fillet or chump end of lamb, trimmed

2 tablespoons rice wine or medium-dry sherry

1 tablespoon soy sauce

1 tablespoon hoisin sauce

1 teaspoon sesame oil

1 teaspoon sugar

1 tablespoon cornflour

2 tablespoons sunflower oil

2.5cm (1 inch) knob of fresh ginger, shredded

2 cloves garlic, sliced

2 red chillies, seeded and chopped

a bunch of spring onions, cut into short lengths

a small handful of chopped coriander leaves

salt

freshly ground black pepper

1. Cut the lamb into small thin pieces. Place in a shallow dish and season with salt and pepper. Add the rice wine or sherry, soy sauce, hoisin sauce, sesame oil, sugar and cornflour. Mix well to coat evenly and leave to marinate for 20 minutes.

2. Heat the sunflower oil in a wok or large frying pan. Add the ginger, garlic and chillies and fry for 30 seconds until fragrant. Stir in the lamb and fry over a high heat until brown, about 4–5 minutes. Add the spring onions and coriander and toss to combine. You may need to add a splash of water. Adjust the seasoning and serve immediately.

Minced Lamb with Spicy Bean Sauce

THIS SPICY meat sauce goes very well with plain boiled rice, tossed with noodles or even with baked potatoes. Pork can be used instead of lamb. Toban sauce is a thick, spicy paste made from garlic, chillies and fermented brown soy beans.

—— SERVES 4 ——

1 tablespoon sunflower oil
1 onion, chopped
2 cloves garlic, chopped
1 tablespoon chopped fresh ginger
450g (1lb) minced lamb
1 tablespoon toban sauce
2 tablespoons soy sauce
1 teaspoon sugar
1 tablespoon rice wine or medium-dry sherry

250ml (8fl oz) chicken stock (see page 32) or water
2 teaspoons cornflour
2 tablespoons chopped coriander leaves
2 tablespoons chopped spring onions
salt
freshly ground black pepper

1. Heat the oil in a wok or large frying pan. Add the onion, garlic and ginger and fry for 2 minutes. Add the lamb, season with salt and pepper and continue to fry for a further 2 minutes. Add the toban sauce, soy sauce, sugar and rice wine or sherry. Stir to mix.

2. Add the stock or water and bring to a quick boil. Remove any scum, then cover and simmer for about 10 minutes or until the lamb is tender. You may need to add more liquid.

3. Blend the cornflour to a paste with 1 tablespoon water and stir into the lamb until the mixture thickens. Taste for seasoning. Finally add the coriander and spring onions.

Tenderloin of Lamb with Plum Sauce

THIS IS great for entertaining. You can seal the lamb beforehand and have all your vegetables ready. Then it is just a matter of putting the lamb in the oven and stir-frying the vegetables. Serve with rice, noodles or potatoes.

—— SERVES 4 ——

3 tablespoons sunflower oil

4 loin of lamb fillets, each weighing about 150g (5oz)

6 tablespoons plum sauce

2 cloves garlic

1 tablespoon chopped fresh ginger

1 red onion, sliced

115g (4oz) baby sweetcorn

1 red pepper, seeded and cut into strips

1 yellow pepper, cut into strips

115g (4oz) mangetout, trimmed

115g (4oz) bean sprouts

a bunch of spring onions, cut into 5cm (2 inch) lengths

2 tablespoons light soy sauce

1 tablespoon dry sherry

4 tablespoons coriander leaves

salt

freshly ground black pepper

——————— ◆ ———————

1. Preheat the oven to 200°C/400°F/Gas 6.

2. Heat 1 tablespoon of the oil in a medium-sized frying pan. Season the lamb fillets with salt and pepper, place them in the hot pan and seal and brown them all over, about 3–5 minutes. Spread with 2 tablespoons of the plum sauce and place in the oven for about 7–10 minutes, or until done to your liking.

3. Meanwhile, heat the remaining oil in a wok or large frying pan. Add the garlic and ginger and fry for 30 seconds. Add the onion and baby sweetcorn and stir-fry for 2 minutes. Add the peppers and mangetout and fry for 4–5 minutes or until the vegetables are tender but still crisp – you may need to add a splash of water. Add the bean sprouts and spring onions and toss. Finally, stir in the soy sauce, sherry and remaining plum sauce and mix well.

4. Serve the lamb sliced or whole on the vegetables, garnished with coriander.

Peppered Lamb Cutlets

THIS IS ONE of my favourite lamb recipes. I like to use a whole rack of lamb – it obviously takes much longer to cook, but it makes a wonderful dinner party dish.

—— SERVES 4 ——

1 tablespoon hoisin sauce
1 tablespoon rice wine or medium-
  dry sherry
3 tablespoons sunflower oil
juice of ½ orange
1 teaspoon grated fresh ginger
2 cloves garlic, chopped

8–12 lamb cutlets, trimmed
1 tablespoon Szechuan
  peppercorns
1 tablespoon black peppercorns
1 tablespoon white peppercorns
1 tablespoon fennel seeds

—————— ◆ ——————

1. Combine the hoisin sauce, rice wine or sherry, 1 tablespoon of the oil, orange juice, ginger and garlic and mix with the lamb cutlets.

2. Dry roast the Szechuan, black and white peppercorns with the fennel seeds in a small pan for 3–4 minutes until fragrant. Coarsely grind the mixture with a pestle and mortar.

3. Heat the remaining oil in a frying pan until very hot. Remove the cutlets from the marinade and reserve any excess. Fry the cutlets on both sides until brown and done to your liking.

4. Spread the pepper mixture on a plate. Take the cutlets from the pan and press them on to the mixture. Deglaze the pan by adding a splash of water and any remaining marinade and stirring to scrape up any sediment and juices at the bottom of the pan. Bring to the boil. Serve the pan juices with the lamb.

VEGETABLES AND TOFU

MANY MAIN dishes of fish and meat include vegetables as supplementary ingredients, but a well-balanced Chinese meal will nevertheless nearly always include a vegetable dish in its own right.

Give vegetables the same respect that you give to fish, chicken and meat. Choose the freshest vegetables in season and look for ones that are firm, crisp and fresh smelling. Most vegetables are prime candidates for stir-frying as it preserves their flavours, textures, colours and natural goodness. Some Chinese vegetables may be hard to find outside Chinese food stores, so improvise with local ones if you can't find them.

Tofu is now widely available in supermarkets. Apart from its nutritional value, it is also versatile and can be stir-fried, braised, stuffed, deep-fried and added to soups and casseroles. Lovers of tofu go into raptures about is slippery, silken texture, although other people may turn their noses up at its blandness. Because it has a mild flavour, it tends to take on the taste and seasoning of the ingredients it is cooked with.

Stir-Fried Cabbage with Ginger and Dried Shrimps

THERE ARE several types of cabbage to choose from, but whether you select a Chinese, Savoy or white variety, you'll be amazed how sweet and tasty this dish is. For vegetarians, you can leave out the dried shrimps.

—— SERVES 4 ——

25g (1oz) dried shrimps
2 tablespoons groundnut oil
2 cloves garlic, crushed
1 tablespoon chopped fresh ginger
1 medium-sized cabbage, shredded
1 small red pepper, seeded and
finely sliced

2 teaspoons cornflour
120ml (4fl oz) chicken stock (see
page 32)
2 tablespoons light soy sauce
1 teaspoon sugar
2 spring onions, cut diagonally into
slices

1. Soak the dried shrimps in warm water for 10 minutes, then drain.

2. Heat the oil in a wok or large frying pan. Add the garlic, ginger and dried shrimps and stir-fry until fragrant. Add the cabbage and stir-fry until it is just wilted. Add the red pepper, toss and cook for a further 2–4 minutes.

3. Blend the cornflour with the stock, soy sauce and sugar. Add to the pan and stir until the mixture boils and thickens. Stir in the spring onions.

Glazed Green Beans with Yellow Bean Sauce

THIS IS A lovely way to cook green beans as the fermented yellow beans complement them and give them a savoury, almost meaty, flavour. Fermented yellow beans are made from soy beans and come in small jars or tins. Once open, it is best to store them in the refrigerator. They are good used in stir-fries. Serve this dish as part of a Chinese meal.

—— SERVES 4 ——

350g (12oz) fine green beans
1 tablespoon fermented yellow
   beans
½ teaspoon sugar
2 tablespoons sunflower oil
1 teaspoon chopped garlic

1 teaspoon chopped fresh ginger
2 shallots, chopped
1 tablespoon rice wine or medium-
   dry sherry
2 teaspoons soy sauce

1. Trim the ends of the green beans and cut the beans diagonally in half.

2. Grind the fermented yellow beans with the sugar.

3. Heat the oil in a wok or large frying pan. Add the garlic, ginger and shallots and fry for 30 seconds. Stir in the yellow bean paste and then the green beans and stir-fry for about 1 minute. Add the rice wine or sherry, soy sauce and 90ml (3fl oz) water. Cover and cook for about 4–5 minutes or until the beans are tender and the liquid has reduced to a glaze.

Lettuce with Oyster Sauce

LETTUCE IS seldom eaten raw in China. It is often stir-fried as a vegetable to accompany other dishes.

—— SERVES 4–6 ——

1 large iceberg or cos lettuce
2 tablespoons groundnut oil

2 tablespoons oyster sauce
salt

1. Separate the lettuce leaves, discarding any bruised or old bits. Tear or cut the larger leaves in half.

2. Bring 250ml (8fl oz) water to the boil and add a good pinch of salt and 1 tablespoon of the oil. Add half the lettuce and, when it starts to wilt, push it to one side and add the remaining lettuce. Give the leaves a couple of stirs – it will only take a few minutes for them to cook.

3. Drain the leaves and toss them with the remaining oil. Turn them on to a dish and drizzle with the oyster sauce.

Stir-Fried Vegetables

VEGETABLES cooked in the Chinese way are crisp and colourful. Any vegetables can be used – just keep them the same size and cook the harder varieties before adding the softer, leafy vegetables, so that they are all ready at the same time.

—— SERVES 4–6 ——

1 small head of mustard greens or
   spring greens
2 celery sticks
1 head of broccoli
2 tablespoons groundnut oil
1 tablespoon finely chopped fresh
   ginger

1 onion, sliced
115g (4oz) mangetout, trimmed
120ml (4fl oz) chicken stock (see
   page 32) or water
salt

———— ◆ ————

1. Cut the mustard greens or spring greens and the celery sticks into sections and separate the broccoli into florets. Keep them more or less the same size and shape.

2. Heat the oil in a wok or large frying pan and add the ginger, cabbage sections, broccoli florets and onion. Stir gently and cook for 2 minutes. Add the celery and mangetout and toss together.

3. Stir in the stock or water and bring to the boil. Cover, and cook until the vegetables are tender, about 3 minutes. Add salt to taste, and serve.

Aubergines with Minced Beef and Toban Sauce

TOBAN SAUCE is a spicy, garlicky bean paste. Usually sold in jars, it is a very popular ingredient in Szechuan cooking. If you can't find it, you can mash together 2 cloves garlic with 1–2 chopped chillies and 2 tablespoons crushed fermented yellow beans.

— SERVES 4 —

657g (1½lb) aubergines
4 tablespoons sunflower oil
175g (6oz) minced beef
1–2 tablespoons toban sauce
250ml (8fl oz) chicken stock (see page 32) or water
2 tablespoons rice wine or medium-dry sherry

1 teaspoon light soy sauce
1 tablespoon dark soy sauce
1 teaspoon sugar
1 teaspoon sesame oil
2 spring onions, finely chopped
salt
freshly ground black pepper

1. Cut the aubergines into sections about 5cm (2 inches) long and 1 cm (½ inch) wide.

2. Heat 2 tablespoons of the sunflower oil in a wok or large frying pan until very hot, then add the aubergines and stir-fry until softened, about 5 minutes. Remove and set aside.

3. Heat the remaining oil in the same pan and add the minced beef and toban sauce and fry for about 5 minutes, stirring to separate the meat. Add the stock or water and simmer for about 10 minutes or until the meat is tender.

4. Return the aubergines to the pan and add the rice wine or sherry, soy sauces, sugar and sesame oil. Cover and cook slowly for another 7–8 minutes. You may need to add more liquid. Check for seasoning and add salt and pepper to taste. Sprinkle with the spring onions and serve.

Stir-Fried Broccoli

You CAN use Chinese broccoli if you happen to shop at a Chinese super-market, otherwise use ordinary broccoli. This is a simple, easy and quick-to-cook recipe.

—— SERVES 4 ——

450g (1lb) broccoli
2 tablespoons groundnut oil
2 cloves garlic, crushed

2 slices of fresh ginger, crushed
1 teaspoon sesame oil
salt

————— ✦ —————

1. Separate the broccoli heads into florets and peel and slice the stalks.

2. Heat the groundnut oil in a wok or large frying pan. Add the garlic, ginger and broccoli and stir-fry for about 1 minute, then add a splash of water and season with a little salt. Cover with a lid and cook for 4–5 minutes or until the broccoli is tender and most of the water has evaporated. Remove the lid, add the sesame oil and continue to stir-fry for a further 30 seconds.

OPPOSITE Chicken with Honey, Ginger and Sweet Chilli Sauce (page 68) served with Stir-Fried Broccoli (page 106) and Boiled Rice (page 115)

Creamed Chinese Cabbage

UNLIKE OTHER Chinese vegetables, the cabbage in this recipe is better overcooked than undercooked. For vegetarians, omit the ham and use vegetable stock instead of chicken stock.

—— SERVES 4–6 ——

1 small Chinese cabbage, about 675g (1½lb)
2 tablespoons sunflower oil
250ml (8fl oz) chicken stock (see page 32) or water

1 tablespoon cornflour
120ml (4fl oz) single cream
2 slices of smoked ham, chopped
salt
freshly ground black pepper

1. Cut the cabbage into 2.5cm (1 inch) sections.

2. Heat the oil in a wok or large frying pan, then add the cabbage and stir-fry for 2 minutes. Season with salt and pepper. Add the stock or water, bring to a quick boil, then cover and cook for about 5 minutes until the cabbage is softened.

3. Dissolve the cornflour in the cream and stir gently into the cabbage until it thickens. Cook gently for another 2–3 minutes. Adjust the seasoning.

4. Sprinkle with the ham and serve hot.

OPPOSITE Wok-Seared Scallops with Asparagus (page 60) and Crispy Seaweed (page 29)

Sesame Courgettes

COURGETTES can taste watery and bland. Cooked this way they are full of flavour and texture.

—— SERVES 4 ——

2 tablespoons sesame seeds
450g (1lb) courgettes
2 tablespoons groundnut oil
10 Szechuan peppercorns (optional)
2 dried chillies, seeded and
   chopped
1 tablespoon chopped fresh ginger
2 cloves garlic, crushed

1 tablespoon rice vinegar
1 tablespoon soy sauce
2 teaspoons sugar
2 spring onions, chopped
1 teaspoon sesame oil
salt
freshly ground black pepper

—— ◆ ——

1. Dry roast the sesame seeds in a small pan for 2–3 minutes until they turn golden and give off a fragrant aroma.

2. Cut the courgettes into 1cm (1/2 inch) thick slices.

3. Heat the groundnut oil in a wok or large frying pan. Add the Szechuan peppercorns, if using, and the chillies and fry for 30 seconds until fragrant. Add the ginger and garlic and fry for a further 30 seconds.

4. Add the courgettes and stir-fry for 1–2 minutes. Add the vinegar, soy sauce and sugar. Toss well and cook for a further 5–6 minutes or until the courgettes are tender but still crisp.

5. Check for seasoning and add salt and pepper to taste. Add the sesame seeds, spring onions and sesame oil.

Vegetable Fritters

I HAVE SEEN many chefs and lecturers making these at various times. Very often, they turn out as soggy blobs. My good friend Sharon has the lightest touch when it comes to frying. Her secret lies in the use of a thin batter.

—— SERVES 4 ——

1 courgette
1 aubergine
115g (4oz) cauliflower florets
50g (2oz) baby sweetcorn
50g (2oz) button mushrooms
1 egg
1 teaspoon vinegar

115g (4oz) self-raising flour
2 tablespoons chopped coriander
    leaves
oil for deep frying
sweet chilli sauce
salt

1. Cut the courgette into 5cm (2 inch) lengths, then cut each length lengthways into 4–6 sections. Cut the aubergine into similar sizes and shapes. The cauliflower florets, baby sweetcorn and button mushrooms won't need any special preparation.

2. Whisk 150ml (5fl oz) water with the egg, vinegar, flour and a pinch of salt, then stir in the coriander.

3. Heat the oil. Working in batches, dip the vegetables into the batter and fry until crisp and golden brown. Remove each batch with a slotted spoon, drain on absorbent kitchen paper and keep warm in a low oven. Serve with sweet chilli sauce.

Sweet and Sour Cucumber

LIGHT AND refreshing, this can be served as a salad, or as a pickle to accompany fried dishes.

—— SERVES 4 ——

1 cucumber
2 tablespoons sugar
3 tablespoons rice vinegar

1 teaspoon chopped fresh ginger
1 teaspoon sesame oil (optional)
salt

1. Finely slice the cucumber, sprinkle with salt and leave for about 10 minutes. Rinse if necessary and drain well.

2. Dissolve the sugar in the vinegar and toss the cucumber with the dressing. Sprinkle with the ginger and drizzle with the sesame oil, if using.

Braised Tofu

Tofu, also known as bean curd, is easily available these days. Made from soy beans, it is high in nutrients, and has been an important part of oriental diets for many years. Its neutral flavour lends itself beautifully to strong seasonings such as miso – another product made from the versatile soy bean. Serve this dish on a bed of leafy greens.

—— SERVES 4 ——

675 (1½lb) firm tofu
150ml (5fl oz) chicken stock (see
   page 32) or water
1 tablespoon dark soy sauce
1 tablespoon dark miso
1 teaspoon sugar
1 teaspoon cornflour
4 tablespoons groundnut oil

1 teaspoon chopped garlic
1 tablespoon chopped fresh ginger
2 dried chillies, flaked
1 teaspoon sesame oil
2 spring onions, cut into short
   lengths
salt
freshly ground black pepper

1. Cut the tofu into 2.5cm (1 inch) cubes.

2. Combine the stock or water, soy sauce, miso, sugar and cornflour.

3. Heat 3 tablespoons of the groundnut oil in a wok or large frying pan, then add the tofu and fry for 1–2 minutes on each side until golden brown. Remove the tofu from the pan and set aside.

4. Wipe the pan clean and heat the remaining oil. Add the garlic, ginger and chillies and stir-fry for 30 seconds. Stir the sauce mixture into the pan and bring to a simmer. Return the tofu to the pan and simmer gently for about 5–6 minutes, season to taste with salt and pepper, then add the sesame oil and spring onions.

Stir-Fried Mixed Peas with Tofu and Cashew Nuts

Pᴇᴀ sʜᴏᴏᴛs are only available for a short time and are often hard to find unless you grow your own peas. But they are great in salads and quick stir-fries. You can leave them out, or perhaps use bean sprouts or watercress instead.

—— Sᴇʀᴠᴇs 4 ——

50g (2oz) cashew nuts
2 tablespoons groundnut oil
1 tablespoon grated fresh ginger
150g (5oz) sugar snap peas
150g (5oz) mangetout, trimmed
300g (10oz) tofu, cut into 2.5cm
  (1 inch) cubes

2 tablespoons light soy sauce
50g (2oz) pea shoots
1 teaspoon sesame oil
salt
freshly ground black pepper

1. Spread out the cashew nuts on a baking tray and roast in an oven preheated to 180°C/350°F/Gas 4 for 10–12 minutes until they turn golden brown.

2. Heat the groundnut oil in a wok or large frying pan. Add the ginger and the sugar snap peas and mangetout and stir-fry for about 1–2 minutes. Add the tofu and soy sauce, cover with a lid and cook for a further 2 minutes. You may need to add a splash of water.

3. Add the pea shoots, cashew nuts and sesame oil and toss over a high heat until the pea shoots are just wilted. Add salt and pepper to taste and serve.

Tofu with Minced Pork in Brown Bean Sauce

THIS IS one of my favourite ways of cooking tofu. It produces a contrast of texture and flavour: whilst the tofu stays soft and silky, it comes with a pungent spicy sauce.

—— SERVES 4 ——

2 tablespoons groundnut oil
2 teaspoons finely chopped garlic
1 tablespoon finely chopped fresh
  ginger
2 dried chillies, seeded and chopped
225g (8oz) minced pork
120ml (4fl oz) chicken stock (see
  page 32)
2 tablespoons soy sauce
1 tablespoon brown bean paste
  (optional)

450g (1lb) tofu, cut into 2.5cm
  (1 inch) cubes
2 teaspoons cornflour
1 teaspoon sesame oil
2 tablespoons chopped spring
  onions
2 red chillies, seeded (optional)
salt
freshly ground black pepper

———— ✦ ————

1. Heat the groundnut oil in a wok or large frying pan. Add the garlic, ginger, dried chillies, minced pork and salt and pepper and stir-fry for 5 minutes. Add the stock, soy sauce and brown bean paste. Stir and bring to the boil, then cover and simmer gently for another 5–7 minutes or until the pork is tender.

2. Add the tofu cubes and turn them over to coat them with the sauce. Cover and leave to cook for a further 5 minutes until the tofu is thoroughly heated through.

3. Blend the cornflour with a little water and stir it into the pork until the mixture thickens. Adjust the seasoning. Finally, add the sesame oil, spring onions and the red chillies, if using.

RICE AND NOODLES

RICE AND noodles provide bulk in the Chinese diet. Noodles are the primary staple in Northern China, whereas rice is preferred in Southern China.

A bowl of plain boiled rice is essential to any meal. Small portions of superbly flavoured dishes are served merely as accompaniments and are used to flavour the rice. The many varieties of rice include long grain and fragrant, short and round, glutinous and black. It is treated with the greatest of respect.

Many different varieties of noodles are eaten in China. They may be thick or thin, flat or round. Most are prepared from hard flour which is mixed to a dough with water and sometimes eggs; others are made from rice flour, mung-bean starch or buckwheat flour. For information on different types of noodle, see page 5.

Noodles are cheap and versatile, quick to prepare and make a nutritious and satisfying one-dish meal. They play a vital role in China's culture as well as its cuisine. They symbolise longevity and are eaten, uncut, at birthday celebrations.

Boiled Rice

Plain boiled rice is to the Chinese what bread is to other people: the indispensable accompaniment to a meal. I always cook more than I need so that I can use what is left over to make fried rice.

—— Serves 4–6 ——

450g (1lb) long grain or jasmine rice
900ml (1½ pints) water

——————— ◆ ———————

1. Place the rice in a saucepan. Fill the pan with cold water and swish the rice around, then rinse and drain. Do this a couple of times.

2. Cover the rice with enough water to come about 2.5cm (1 inch) above the top of the rice.

3. Bring the rice to the boil and cover with a tight-fitting lid. Reduce the heat and simmer gently for about 10 minutes. Turn the heat off completely, and leave the rice to rest and steam in its own heat for another 8–10 minutes. Fluff up the rice with a pair of chopsticks or the back of a wooden spoon before serving.

Basic Fried Rice

FRIED RICE is served more often in the West than in China, where it is served as a filler at the end of a dinner party or banquet, usually without soy sauce. To make fried rice, you have to plan ahead as the rice has to be cooked and thoroughly cooled. This can be done the night before.

—— SERVES 4–6 ——

3 tablespoons sunflower oil
1 onion, chopped
2 eggs, beaten
350g (12oz) long grain rice, cooked
  (cooked weight will be 1kg (2lb
  2oz)

2 tablespoons soy sauce (optional)
salt

———— ◆ ————

1. Heat the sunflower oil in a wok or large frying pan. Add the onion and fry until softened.

2. Add the eggs and once they are just set and lightly scrambled, add the rice. Toss and turn the rice so that it heats through thoroughly. Season with salt and the soy sauce, if using.

Ham, Egg and Prawn Fried Rice

FRIED RICE dishes are popular and, provided you have some cooked rice, are easy to put together and make ideal quick lunch or supper dishes. You can add almost anything to the basic fried rice. As in the previous recipe, the rice must be cooked and completely cold before you begin.

—— SERVES 4–6 ——

2 tablespoons sunflower oil

75g (3oz) button mushrooms, quartered

4 spring onions, cut diagonally

2 eggs, lightly beaten

350g (12oz) long grain rice, cooked (cooked weight will be 1kg/2lb 2oz)

50g (2oz) frozen peas, thawed and drained

115g (4oz) diced ham

115g (4oz) cooked peeled prawns

3 tablespoons light soy sauce

1 tablespoon oyster sauce

1 teaspoon sesame oil (optional)

a small bunch of basil leaves

salt

freshly ground black pepper

—————— ◆ ——————

1. Heat the sunflower oil in a wok or large frying pan. Add the mushrooms and half the spring onions and fry until softened. Push the mixture to one side, pour in the eggs and cook until they are just set and lightly scrambled.

2. Add the rice and fry for about 5–6 minutes. Add the peas, ham and prawns. Toss and continue to fry until the mixture is thoroughly heated through. Add the soy and oyster sauces, the sesame oil, if using, and salt and pepper to taste. Sprinkle with the remaining spring onions and the basil leaves.

Vegetable Fried Rice

You CAN use any vegetables of your choice. This is a good way of using up any left-overs. I sometimes like to vary the taste by adding a couple of spoonfuls of tomato ketchup to the rice and serving it with a fried egg on top.

—— SERVES 4–6 ——

2 tablespoons sunflower oil
2 courgettes, diced
2 celery sticks, sliced
350g (12oz) long grain rice, cooked
  (cooked weight will be 1kg/2lb
  2oz)
1 red pepper, seeded and diced

2 eggs, lightly beaten
115g (4oz) bean sprouts
1 teaspoon sesame oil
2 teaspoons dark soy sauce
2 tablespoons light soy sauce
4 spring onions, chopped

—————— ✦ ——————

1. Heat the sunflower oil in a wok or large frying pan. Add the courgettes and celery and stir-fry for 2 minutes.

2. Add the rice and stir-fry for 1 minute. Add the pepper and stir-fry for a further minute.

3. Make a well in the centre of the rice and stir in the eggs for 30 seconds. When they are half set and scrambled mix them with the rice.

4. Add the bean sprouts and stir in the sesame oil and the dark and light soy sauces. Mix well and sprinkle with the spring onions.

Steamed Chicken and Rice

THIS IS ONE of my favourite meals, served on its own or with some greens. The chicken is silky and tender, and the rice is tasty. You can cook and serve this in individual clay pots. Other popular variations combine rice with pork spare ribs and black beans, or with wind- or air-dried meat and salted ducks' eggs.

—— SERVES 4 ——

450g (1lb) boneless chicken pieces
1 tablespoon rice wine or medium-
 dry sherry
1 tablespoon light soy sauce, plus
 extra for serving
1 teaspoon sugar
1 teaspoon cornflour
a few shakes of sesame oil
350g (12oz) long grain rice
900ml (1½pints) chicken stock (see
 page 32) or water

4 dried shiitake mushrooms, soaked
 (see page 5) and finely sliced
1 tablespoon finely shredded fresh
 ginger
4 tablespoons finely chopped spring
 onions
salt
freshly ground black pepper

—————— ◆ ——————

1. Cut the chicken into bite-sized pieces. Put these into a bowl, then add the rice wine or sherry, soy sauce, sugar, cornflour and sesame oil and mix well.

2. Wash and drain the rice. Combine it with the stock or water and bring to the boil. Turn the heat to low and continue to cook for another 6–7 minutes or until most of the liquid has evaporated.

3. Mix the chicken with the mushrooms, ginger and 2 tablespoons of the spring onions and sprinkle over the rice. Cover and continue to cook for a further 7 minutes. Turn the heat off completely and let the rice rest undisturbed for another 10 minutes. Just before serving add a little pepper and sprinkle with the remaining spring onions. Serve with soy sauce.

Soft Fried Noodles

THIS IS A simple noodle dish to serve instead of other starches like rice and potatoes. Chinese egg (and wheat) noodles do not require as much cooking as Italian pasta and therefore make the ideal base for speedy meals.

—— SERVES 4 ——

350g (12oz) thin dried egg noodles
2 tablespoons vegetable oil
2 tablespoons chopped spring
  onions

1 teaspoon sesame oil
2 tablespoons soy sauce (optional)
salt

—————— ◆ ——————

1. Bring a large pan of water to the boil. Add the noodles, then remove the pan from the heat and leave for 3–5 minutes, depending on the thickness of the noodles. Stir and loosen them with a pair of chopsticks or the back of a wooden spoon. Drain the noodles and rinse them in cold running water. Drain them again.

2. Heat the vegetable oil in a wok or large frying pan, then add the spring onions and fry for 30 seconds. Add the noodles and a pinch of salt, stir gently to separate the strands and fry the noodles until heated through. If you like them slightly crisp, turn up the heat and fry a little bit longer. Stir in the sesame oil and the soy sauce, if using.

Crisp Noodle Cake

THIS IS A SIMPLE accompaniment for all the main dishes in this book. You can make a large cake and cut it into wedges or small individual ones.

—— SERVES 4 ——

350g (12oz) fresh fine egg noodles
4 tablespoons groundnut oil, plus
   extra for tossing (optional)

salt

——— ◆ ———

1. Bring a large pan of water to the boil. Add the noodles and keep the water boiling vigorously.

2. Stir the noodles from the bottom from time to time and cook until they are barely done. This will take about 1–2 minutes – fresh noodles don't take long.

3. Drain the noodles and rinse them in cold running water. Drain them again. If you are not going to use them immediately, it is worth tossing them in a little oil to prevent them from sticking.

4. Heat about 1 tablespoon of the oil in a small frying pan. Arrange the noodles in the pan, spreading them out like a thick pancake. Season with a little salt. Let the cake sizzle and brown, then turn it over and cook the other side. Add more oil as you need it. The cake should be crisp and brown on the outside but soft in the middle. Remove from the pan, keep warm in a low oven and use as required.

Chow Mein

CHOW MEIN means stir-fried noodles. Like fried rice, you can add almost anything to it – vegetables, meat and seafood, the combinations are endless. You can use thick or thin noodles. It is quick and a favourite with everyone.

—— SERVES 4 ——

350g (12oz) dried medium-thick
  wheat noodles
3 tablespoons sunflower oil
2 cloves garlic, crushed and
  chopped
4 slices of fresh ginger, shredded
115g (4oz) chicken breast or pork,
  finely sliced
12 tiger prawns, shelled and
  deveined

115g (4oz) mangetout, trimmed and
  halved
175g (6oz) bean sprouts
50g (2oz) garlic chives (optional)
2 tablespoons soy sauce
2 tablespoons oyster sauce
2 spring onions, cut diagonally
salt
freshly ground black pepper

1. Drop the noodles into a pan of boiling water. Turn off the heat, cover the pan and leave for 3 minutes. Then remove the lid and stir the noodles with a pair of chopsticks or the back of a wooden spoon to loosen them. Drain and rinse under cold running water. Drain again.

2. Heat 1½ tablespoons of the oil until very hot. Add the garlic and ginger and stir-fry for 30 seconds. Add the chicken or pork and prawns and stir-fry for 1–2 minutes or until cooked. Remove from the pan and set aside.

3. Wipe the pan clean and heat the remaining oil. Add the mangetout, bean sprouts and the garlic chives, if using, and stir-fry until the vegetables lose their rawness and start to wilt. Add the noodles and toss and stir them gently to separate. Add the soy and oyster sauces and season with salt and pepper.

4. Add the chicken or pork mixture to the noodles and toss until everything is well mixed. Garnish with the spring onions and serve immediately.

Sesame Pasta Quills

THIS IS A simple dish to serve as an alternative to rice and other starches. It goes very well with rich savoury dishes like Red or Soy Chicken (see page 73) or Braised Pork Chops (see page 90).

—— SERVES 4 ——

2 tablespoons sesame seeds
225g (8oz) penne
4 spring onions, chopped
1 tablespoon groundnut oil

1 teaspoon sesame oil
salt
freshly ground black pepper

1. Dry roast the sesame seeds in a small pan for 2–3 minutes until they turn golden and give off a fragrant aroma.

2. Cook the penne in a large pan of boiling salted water according to the instructions on the packet.

3. Drain the penne, return them to the pan and toss with the remaining ingredients.

Singapore Noodles

THERE ARE numerous versions of this popular noodle dish. As its name implies, it originated in Singapore. Rice vermicelli are stir-fried with ham, prawns, vegetables and a hint of curry powder.

—— **S ERVES 4** ——

375g (13oz) rice vermicelli noodles
3 tablespoons rice vinegar
4 tablespoons light soy sauce
½ teaspoon sugar
½ teaspoon chilli paste
3 tablespoons groundnut oil
1 tablespoon curry powder
1 tablespoon chopped garlic
1 tablespoon chopped fresh ginger
1 red pepper, seeded and finely
   sliced
175g (6oz) cooked peeled prawns

115g (4oz) sliced ham, shredded
350g (12oz) bean sprouts
50g (2oz) frozen peas, thawed and
   drained
4 spring onions, cut diagonally
4 tablespoons roughly chopped
   coriander leaves
2 red chillies, seeded and finely
   sliced
salt
freshly ground black pepper

———— ◆ ————

1. Soak the rice vermicelli in hot water for about 10–15 minutes until softened. Drain.

2. Combine the vinegar, soy sauce, sugar and chilli paste.

3. Heat the oil in a wok or large, preferably non-stick, frying pan. Add the curry powder, garlic and ginger and stir-fry for 10 seconds. Add the pepper and stir-fry for 1 minute. Add the rice vermicelli and cook, stirring, for about 5 minutes. Add the prawns, ham, bean sprouts, peas and soy sauce mixture.

4. Toss and fry until the vermicelli are tender and the rest of the ingredients heated through and well mixed in. Check for seasoning and add salt and pepper to taste. Add the spring onions. Transfer the vermicelli to a serving dish and garnish with the coriander and red chillies.

Spicy Szechuan Noodles

AN EXCELLENT noodle salad to serve as a starter or a light lunch. For vegetarians, omit the chicken and use vegetable instead of chicken stock.

—— SERVES 4–6 ——

1/4 teaspoon Szechuan peppercorns
450g (1lb) thick wheat noodles
2 tablespoons peanut butter
1 tablespoon soy sauce
1 tablespoon rice vinegar
2 tablespoons sweet chilli sauce
4 tablespoons chicken stock (see page 32)
2 tablespoons groundnut oil

1 tablespoon sesame oil
225g (8oz) cooked chicken, shredded
4 spring onions, chopped
50g (2oz) peanuts, roasted and roughly chopped
2 tablespoons coriander leaves
salt

1. Dry roast the Szechuan peppercorns by heating in a small pan for 3–4 minutes until fragrant. Leave to cool and then grind with a pestle and mortar.

2. Cook the noodles in a large pan of boiling water, according to the instructions on the packet. Drain them and rinse in cold running water. Drain them again and set aside.

3. Combine the peanut butter, Szechuan peppercorns, soy sauce, vinegar, sweet chilli sauce, stock and groundnut and sesame oils in a large serving bowl.

4. Add the noodles, chicken and spring onions and toss until they are evenly coated with the dressing. Add salt to taste then sprinkle with the peanuts and coriander.

Linguine with Cucumber, Bean Sprouts and Sesame Sauce

CHINESE SESAME paste is made from ground roasted sesame seeds and is quite different in taste to tahini, the Middle Eastern version. Use smooth peanut butter if sesame paste is unavailable. Spaghetti or angel hair pasta can be substituted for the linguine.

—— SERVES 4 ——

½ cucumber
2 cloves garlic, finely chopped
2 tablespoons Chinese sesame paste
3 tablespoons soy sauce
2 tablespoons rice wine or medium-
  dry sherry
2–3 tablespoons rice vinegar
1 teaspoon sugar
½ teaspoon chilli sauce
350g (12oz) linguine pasta

4 spring onions, chopped
175g (6oz) bean sprouts
2 tablespoons roasted unsalted
  peanuts, roughly chopped
  (optional)
2 red chillies, seeded and sliced
2 tablespoons coriander leaves
salt
freshly ground black pepper

1. Cut the cucumber in half lengthways and remove and discard the seeds. Slice the flesh into fine strips about 5cm (2 inches) long.

2. In a bowl, combine the garlic, sesame paste, soy sauce, rice wine or sherry, vinegar, sugar and chilli sauce. Mix well.

3. Cook the linguine according to the instructions on the packet until tender. Drain immediately and toss with the sauce and the spring onions. Check for seasoning and add salt and pepper to taste.

4. Garnish the linguine with the cucumber, bean sprouts, peanuts, if using, chillies and coriander.

DESSERTS

As a rule, the Chinese prefer savouries to sweets. Desserts as such are unknown and do not accompany family meals. On occasions, fresh fruit may be served after a meal. Most Chinese restaurants offer very little for dessert other than fruits, sorbet or ice cream.

Knowing how Westerners like to finish off a meal with something sweet, I have included a short selection of recipes based on fruit. Some are served hot or warm, and others cold. And there is, of course, no reason at all why you couldn't serve your favourite dessert after a Chinese meal.

Poached Loquats with Kirsch

LOQUATS originated in China and are related to apples, pears and European medlars. They have a distinctive taste, both acid and sweet, with juicy, yellow to apricot coloured flesh.

—— SERVES 4 ——

12–16 loquats depending on size
225g (8oz) sugar
2 strips of lemon peel
juice of ½ lemon

2 tablespoons Kirsch
150ml (5fl oz) Greek yogurt or thick
pouring cream

——— ◆ ———

1. Peel the loquats.

2. Put the sugar, lemon strips, lemon juice and 500ml (16fl oz) water in a pan and stir over a medium heat until the sugar dissolves. Bring to the boil, add the loquats and poach them over a low heat for about 10 minutes or until they are tender. Cool the loquats in the syrup.

3. Transfer the loquats into serving bowls and drizzle with the Kirsch and some of the syrup. Serve with Greek yogurt or thick pouring cream.

Melon in Ginger Wine

Choose melons of different varieties and colours. You can scoop the flesh into balls with a melon baller and serve them in glasses with fresh mint – it will look stunning.

—— Serves 4 ——

60ml (2fl oz) ginger wine
2 tablespoons sugar
2 pieces of preserved ginger, finely
   shredded

2 small melons
4 sprigs of mint

1. Put the ginger wine, sugar and 120ml (4fl oz) water in a pan and stir over a medium heat until the sugar dissolves. Add the shredded ginger. Remove from the heat and leave to cool.

2. Cut the melons into halves and scoop out the seeds. Cut the flesh into segments and place in a dish. Pour the syrup over the melon and leave in a cool place or refrigerator until ready to serve. Garnish with the mint.

Steamed Honeyed Pears

A SOOTHING, simple and excellent dessert.

—— SERVES 4 ——

4 large pears
4 tablespoons honey

———————— ◆ ————————

1. Cut the tops off the pears, about 2.5cm (1 inch) down, and set them aside. Use a fruit corer or teaspoon to make a deep cavity in each pear, taking care not to puncture the skin or go right through the base.

2. Fill each cavity with honey and replace the tops.

3. Stand the pears upright in individual heatproof dishes or cocottes. Put the dishes in a steamer and steam over simmering water until the pears are tender, about 15–20 minutes depending on their size and ripeness. Serve hot.

Banana Fritters

You will find this very popular snack all over the Far East. The bananas are often glazed with honey or coated with caramel. Try using other fruits such as apples and pineapples.

— SERVES 4 —

115g (4oz) self-raising flour
1 egg
1 tablespoon sesame seeds or
  desiccated coconut

4 large bananas
cornflour for coating
oil for deep frying
icing sugar or ice cream

1. Combine the flour, egg and 150ml (5fl oz) water in a bowl. Mix to a smooth batter. Stir in the sesame seeds or desiccated coconut.

2. Peel the bananas and cut each one into three pieces. Roll lightly in the cornflour.

3. Heat the oil. Working in batches, dip the banana pieces in the batter and drop them into the hot oil. Deep-fry until golden brown. Remove with a slotted spoon and drain on absorbent kitchen paper. Serve hot with a dusting of icing sugar or with ice cream.

Wonton and Ice Cream Tower

THIS IS a very quick and easy dessert to put together. You can serve it with fruit if you wish.

—— SERVES 4 ——

oil for deep frying   8 scoops of ice cream
12 wonton wrappers   icing sugar

———————— ◆ ————————

1. Heat the oil in a deep fryer or wok. Slide in a few wonton wrappers and fry until they expand and turn golden. Remove and drain on absorbent kitchen paper. Repeat with the remaining wrappers.

2. Place a wonton wrapper on each plate and put a scoop of ice cream on top. Repeat this procedure once again and finish with a third wanton wrapper. Dust with the icing sugar and serve immediately.

Poached Peaches in Cinnamon Ginger Syrup

Firm, slightly under-ripe peaches are best for poaching as they will not disintegrate while cooking. I usually make slightly more than I need and serve any that are left over for breakfast, with a few berries.

—— Serves 4–6 ——

115g (4oz) sugar
1 lemon, cut in half
1 stick of cinnamon
2.5cm (1 inch) knob of fresh ginger, crushed and sliced

8 peaches
Greek yogurt or ice cream (optional)

1. Put the sugar, lemon, cinnamon, ginger and 500ml (16fl oz) water in a pan and heat until boiling, then simmer for 5 minutes.

2. Cut the peaches in half and remove the stones. Add them to the syrup and simmer for 5–7 minutes or until tender. Remove the peaches with a slotted spoon.

3. Remove the lemon, cinnamon and ginger from the syrup. Return the syrup to the heat and boil until it is reduced by half. Cool slightly, then pour it over the peaches.

4. Serve the peaches warm or cold, on their own or with Greek yogurt or ice cream.

INDEX